THE BIG LIFE

THE BIG LIFE

Embrace your mess, work your side hustle,
find a monumental relationship, and become
the badass babe you were meant to be

ANN SHOKET

RODALE.

Rodale books may be purchased for business or promotional use or for special sales. For information, please write to: Special Markets Department, Rodale Inc., 733 Third Avenue, New York, NY 10017

Printed in the United States of America
Rodale Inc. makes every effort to use acid-free ⊗, recycled paper ☺.

Photographs by Anne Menke
Book design by Yeon Kim

Library of Congress Cataloging-in-Publication Data
is on file with the Publisher.

ISBN-13: 978-1-62336-824-1 hardcover

Distributed to the trade by Macmillan

2 4 6 8 10 9 7 5 3 1 hardcover

We inspire health, healing, happiness, and love in the world.
Starting with you.

For Richard,
whose eyes light up.

CONTENTS

FOREWORD

Ann and I met during what was probably the single most pivotal and terrifying time of my life. It was 2008 and I had just quit my waitressing job to focus on my YouTube channel full-time. The economy had just crashed and I was a struggling college student. I couldn't let my circumstances limit me, but I was eager to help keep the family financially stable since my mom had been raising us on her own. I had always felt a strong passion for beauty and loved how wearing makeup can transform people from within. Wanting to provide that experience for other women, I applied to several department store beauty counters, but was rejected because I didn't have sales experience. This defining moment could have led me away from my dreams; instead, it inspired me to open another door: a laptop.

It seemed that the universe had a different path for me; the low-quality videos I'd shot on my webcam proved to be the beginning of my career in beauty. In 2007, I posted my first video on YouTube—and garnered 40,000 views within a week. Subscribers began asking for insight on everything from perfecting a smoky eye to creating a flawless complexion. I responded with countless videos providing a guide to coveted beauty looks. This interactive dynamic between me and my followers formed the basis of a powerful, growing community and a new way of sharing information. Women all across the world were connecting in an authentic way, and I felt that it was my duty to continue the conversation. Making the radical decision to pursue my YouTube channel full-time completely changed the path that I was on, and through that leap of faith, I rediscovered the dreams that had been the real driving force within me all along. It was the first time that I felt I had a sense of power in the world.

Every day, the question "Am I doing enough?" is on almost every 20- and 30-year-old's mind. More than ever, women can choose what path is right for us. But is it becoming too much? Has the dream of "having it all" gone from an aspiration to a requirement in today's world? These days, the pressures of getting into a good college, acing that job interview, entering a relationship, and beyond, constantly weigh us down. We all have a different purpose in life, but we can easily get wrapped up in expectations along the way. I, too, have felt these pressures and found myself searching for clarity in the confusion and yearning for a simpler, purer frame of mind.

As a little girl, I dreamed of saving the world through art. I always believed that art could take people away from sadness and poverty by making the world a more beautiful place. I still remember a diary entry from April 11, 2003 (my 16th birthday!) that says, "My dream is to one day become well known for my art." That was my Big Life in writing. When you are a child, your ambitions and dreams are so pure and true. We all have something special to provide for society, and it's magical when we get the chance to activate this purpose. The key is to continually reconnect your focus and ask yourself, "What am I going to do next? What does it mean? Why does it matter?" These questions light the way toward discovering your true destiny. From the very beginning, art was my guiding light, and it ignited my passion for inspiring and helping others to live more meaningful lives.

Today, the Internet has presented incredible opportunities for women in business; we are on the brink of a golden age. Through blogs, videos, and social media, the Internet has given women all over the world the opportunity to have a voice, build their own careers, and connect with other people, especially within the beauty realm. By sharing new looks and ideas, we have redefined the concept of beauty and transformed it into something much bigger: a diverse and empowering community. This community has provided us with the power of self-expression, and has ultimately developed a positive platform of change for women everywhere. It has shaped the way we regard our opinions, our confidence, and ourselves, and yet this is only the beginning. With this confidence, we can uncover our true potential—and with the right tools, imagine what we can accomplish in the next 50 years! This new definition of *beauty* is the driving force behind everything I have done thus far. I am fortunate to have the opportunity to give back to the community that began this journey, and I feel proud to have played even a small part in building a deeper and more meaningful conversation within the beauty industry. So many young women now have a safe outlet where they can shine their light for the world to see!

Helping women realize their own true potential is what keeps me inspired. That's why I am so honored to be a part of Ann's incredible book and share my Big Life journey with you.

I have so much respect and admiration for Ann; she has redefined her own meaning of *success* by dedicating her powerful
voice to encourage and guide young women throughout her
career. She is a true example of finding your meaning by
embracing the unexpected and listening to your inner voice.
I can only hope that the stories of the powerful, inspiring
women in this book encourage you to pursue your purest
dreams and uncover what you truly value.

Physically, mentally, and emotionally, we evolve through
experience, and we never stop growing.

Good luck!

Michelle Phan

INTRODUCTION

You always knew you'd do big things. Even when you were sitting in your teenage bedroom in some sleepy suburb, you were already plotting the limitless possibilities that life had in store for you. First, you'd move to a bigger city, you imagined. Maybe you'd start a fashion company, revolutionize the tech industry, claim stardom as a digital influencer, shape national policy, find a cure for a massive public health threat, or land a glamorous job in publishing. You could even picture your first apartment—totally Instagram-worthy, even though you'd rarely be there between work, spin classes, networking coffees, and brunch with the squad. You'd plan voluntourism vacations to Nepal, where you'd help create sustainable businesses for local girls and women. There'd be a partner, too, whose eyes would light up when you talked about the delicious possibilities for your life. In that teenage bedroom, you were able to envision a life that was bigger than anything you could see around you.

How do I know? Because I was there fanning the flames of that first spark of inspiration. As the editor-in-chief of *Seventeen* for the better part of a decade, I made it my mission to help you imagine a life that was exciting, fun, and *meaningful*. I helped lead some of the complex conversations that helped you navigate the tricky terrain of adolescence. I have always been your biggest cheerleader.

Those early dreams are a promise you made to yourself. In your teenage bedroom, you vowed that you'd go after every opportunity and not settle for the easy road; you vowed to honor your ambition. And those dreams are the most powerful because, at that moment, you are a blank canvas. You've made no mistakes that can't be fixed, and you are not beholden to one city or one job. Your life is endless possibility. You are pure potential. The biggest disappointment would be not fulfilling the promise of that dream and finding yourself sidetracked by a life that's made small by busy tasks, daily annoyances, and must-dos.

And yet now, as you're putting muscle on the framework of your life, the road ahead is even rockier, and those dreams, which should be closer than ever, can feel hopelessly out of reach.

Fast-forward from those early ideas of who you could be: You got yourself a gig, but your current boss wants you to sit quietly and wait to get promoted; or worse, your boss is that girl who graduated a year ahead of you and is using her new hyperinflated title to make you feel less than. Or maybe you opted for a fun start-up where the title is bigger but the only pay is cool cache. You're not afraid of hustle; in fact, you thrive on it. But it's hard to feel like you're on the path to those dreams when you're still checking your bank balance every time you get a mani and wondering whether the chicks who stayed back home working on their Pinterest wedding boards are better off than you are.

You know you have more to offer than the world is letting

you. But, here is the truth: You are the revolution—you might not see it now, but I do. I've been at the front lines of the changing tastes and values of young women for the past 15 years, and this generation—your generation—is so laser-focused on personal success and achievement in an unprecedented way. Still, I know it's hard to feel like you're leading a revolution when you're just one girl who is desperate to move up or move around in her career. You can still see your dream, but how do you get there when no clear path has been cut for you? Where do you begin when you're feeling itchy for the world to validate your power? When ambition and career are at the center of your life, how do you put together the rest of the pieces?

As part of the research for this book, I have had a series of dinners at my apartment in New York City (though "dinners" might be overselling it—it's fancy frozen pizza and many bottles of rosé). For each dinner, a group of about six or so friends of a friend of a friend has come together to talk about being young, hungry, and ambitious. These women are in their 20s and 30s, originally from different parts of the country, and working in different industries. And yes, they've all hustled to New York—but it hardly matters if we're meeting in Manhattan or a small town in the Midwest. The emotional threads that connect us are stronger than the geography that separates us. No matter where you live or where you work, the quest for the Big Life is just as urgent and just as overwhelming.

The dinners have been attended by a rotating cast, with some women working at giant high-profile companies and some at teeny-tiny start-ups you haven't heard of yet. Some have been on the *Forbes* "30 under 30" list, some are still hustling to get their foot in the door, and some don't even know what kind of career they want to have. But what unites them all is their hunger to craft the Big Life—that delicious cocktail of work, career, respect, ambition, money, and a monumental relationship—on their own terms.

I call these women the Badass Babes because they are the kind of chicks we all want to be: confident and complex. We talk through the itchy emotions around money, sex, dating, love, friends, marriage, and, of course, work. And let's be honest, at the end of the day, over a glass of wine, we're just more likely to talk about what jolts us awake at 4:00 a.m.—to toss aside that perfect Instagrammy, all-high-fives life we've carefully curated to say what's actually on our minds.

I start every Badass Babes dinner with this question: "If I could solve any problem for you, what would it be?" You'd think that there would be hundreds, *thousands,* of possible answers. But after hosting dozens of dinners (and still counting), I can tell you that the same questions come up every single time:

- *How do I find a career that is also my passion?*
- *How do I find a partner who honors my ambition?*
- *How will I be able to have a big, demanding career without taking my foot off the gas when I have children?*
- *How do I get paid what I'm worth?*
- *How do I get the respect I deserve from my bosses?*
- *And finally, will all this struggle be worth it?*

Those are the questions that frame the discussion in this book, and you'll hear from many of the Badass Babes who shared their stories with me.

You'll meet Vanessa, who, after bouncing from internship to internship, finally landed a proper-paying gig and hustled her way up to art director at a prestige beauty company. She loves that she's finally found a job that marries her passion for design and her need to be well paid. But when she was being eyed for a promotion, she didn't gleefully accept. Instead, she found the courage to push back hard and negotiate a custom title and role for herself. From the outside, it looks like she's crushing it, but she's under so much stress that she often finds the loose ends of her life unraveling. She confessed that the eating disorder she had as a teen came back full force under the pressure she feels to be perfect at work.

Savannah is working every angle of her side hustle. She leads by saying she's the editor-in-chief of a cool new website. The thing is, it's so cool and new that there's no revenue, so she has two other gigs that pay the bills. She makes "robocalls" from her apartment for a financial start-up in the morning, heads to her waitressing gig in the early evening, and then goes home to edit pieces from her writers late into the night. And oh, she's training to be a Pilates instructor in her spare time.

You'd be jealous of Jordan's impressive résumé if she wasn't so hilariously self-deprecating. Jordan's life is full and messy—she feels like she's always one project away from dropping the ball at any minute. She fills her life to the point of spilling over because she has something to prove to the doubters who said that a girl from a small blue-collar Midwest town would never amount to much, to the negging boyfriends who diminish her to make themselves feel bigger, and to herself: that she's not the lonely, acne-pocked teen girl who buried her head in her books waiting for a chance to do something more with her life.

Grace loves that her boss calls her a leprechaun because

she's so rare: a millennial woman of color in the C-suite of a major corporation. Her whole life has been headed toward this moment. She has the big job, makes great money, has access to major power players in business, and even has a handsome man with his own equally impressive résumé. But she wakes up at 4:00 a.m. with the nagging feeling that there's something else that could make her happier. A job with less pressure or a big philanthropic role might help, she reasons. Then again, maybe it's a different partner her soul really craves. The worst part is that, for the first time in her life, she doesn't even know where to look for the right answer.

The intimacy of the conversations with these women and dozens of others has helped the advice here evolve from *how-to* to *me-too*. The mission of this book is to create a sisterhood of young women, like you, who are working through the most complex issues in their lives *together*. What follows are not grand pronouncements from a major magazine editor broadcasting her thoughts to a massive audience. It's not even that "big sister" voice that we use as shorthand for someone who has been through it all and wants to tell you how it is. That's not my role. I don't pretend that my story is anything like the one you're writing for yourself. I'm writing this book, not because I have the solutions, but because I have the same fears.

I've been that girl who looked out of her teenage bedroom dreaming of something more, something bigger. I love goals and strategy, but I'm not a huge planner. I didn't graduate college with a 10-year plan to become the editor-in-chief of a legendary brand. I thought I might write novels. And then I thought I might move to San Francisco and launch a dot-com. For a minute I thought I might be a business journalist—I love asking nosy questions! It wasn't until I was several years into my media career that I realized how meaningful I would find it to have deep, emotional, important conversations about how you grow into who you're supposed to be.

The one trademark of my journey is that I always wanted to carve a new path. I am always looking for opportunities to jump into new territory and figure out how to leave my mark. To me, there is nothing worse than feeling like you already know how the story ends. I don't want every day to feel like the one before. I wanted to explore and experience—and I still do.

My version of the Big Life is still a work in progress, but I will happily share some of my quest: how I received a stack of rejection letters when applying for my first magazine job (letters that I still hold on to as a badge of honor); how I threw up before one of my pitch meetings to be editor-in-chief (didn't get the gig) and how I knew I'd aced the next one; why I didn't meet my dream guy until I had the big job under my belt; and how we got married, had two babies, and then (sort of) talked about life, family, and work balance.

The dinners have changed my thinking in many ways. And they have occasionally been a powerful force for change for the women around my dinner table too. One group of Badass Babes has continued the conversation over Bloody Marys at a monthly brunch meet-up. In the middle of a heated conversation about the kinds of partners ambitious women need, one 23-year-old woman realized that her 38-year-old boyfriend had been lovely steady support as she waded through the rough waters of her first big job, but after a year, he was sort of an emotional anchor. The conversation turned to break-up strategies, and she left the dinner with a promise to gently set him free. At a dinner with young superstars who had made headlines in their respective fields before their

30th birthdays, the women spent the first 20 minutes offering contacts and insider info to help one another overcome whatever new hurdle they were facing. The rock-star mom dinner was the shortest—they all had new babies who would be up in a few precious hours—but also the most revealing. These women had clearly spent a lot of time thinking about how they would navigate family and career, but they'd never shared their most personal struggles. And at one dinner, after the third artichoke pizza was served and another bottle of rosé opened, one buttoned-up Badass Babe in the finance department of a company that was struggling to reinvent itself confessed that she secretly wished she could shift gears and work at a nonprofit. Two weeks later, I got a note from her, saying she'd been so moved by the conversation that she'd started applying to nonprofits immediately and landed a coveted business-side gig at a major charity.

I am honored that they've shared their stories with me so candidly, and I have honored their transparency by changing their names and referring to them by using only a first-name pseudonym. The women who are credited by first and last name were all interviewed on the record, and those are their real names.

Ultimately, with having had so many women around my small dining table, there is one bright and shining truth I've discovered: Everyone wants to know that they're not alone in their quest for the Big Life.

Listen, you know that there have been a lot of stories treating "millennial women" as if you were strange creatures to be studied and observed, not powerful women who want to be understood and respected. (Take this recent headline from the *New York Times* business section: "Goldman Sachs Bankers Are Trying to Crack the Secret Habits of a Potentially

Lucrative Species of Retail Shopper: Millennial Women." A *species*?! Way to make a girl feel special!)

I want this book to make you feel like a *badass*. It's that surge you get inside when you're meeting that huge challenge: You're completely in control of your domain, and the world is bending to you—the seas magically part, and all lights are green. When you're being a badass, you feel your true power, and people give you what you want: the custom job title, the lead on a coveted assignment, or the opportunity to step into the spotlight and show the world how brilliant you really are. It's the same bit of magic that you feel when the hottest guy at the bar asks for your number and then texts you the next day. But sometimes this all-empowering feeling gets crushed—by a crap boss, a sabotaging coworker, roommate drama, or a hookup who ghosts, leaving you crying in the bathroom at work. *The Big Life* is about learning to feel like that alluring, totally confident chick all the damn time.

It's my mission to help you recognize your power—and to make the world recognize it too. And if you're worrying whether those dark nights of the soul, all the hard work and awkward situations and complicated itchy emotions around wanting something so big and so badly, will ever be worth it, I'm here to tell you that they will. After all, this is your life . . . and it's going to be *big*.

ANN SHOKET

Be fearless,
try everything
& don't plan too much!

xoxo
- A.

1

THE
BIG LIFE

THAT SEXY COCKTAIL OF CAREER, AMBITION, RESPECT, MONEY, AND A MONUMENTAL RELATIONSHIP

Whether you realize it or not, you are redefining what it means to be powerful and successful in the world. For everyone. Forever.

I've never really known where the conversation will go when I sit down with a new group of women—everyone is at a different place in her journey and has different experiences to share and concerns to discuss. I remember being in awe of one group of women who were true power players. These women had quickly risen to the top of their fields. They've managed to get major funding, disrupt entire industries, and become CEOs of companies they'd created themselves. I was energized by a dinner where many of the women were right out of school or starting their first real jobs. They came to my table bursting with excitement, swapping stories about taking their first steps in the world, and wondering how to conquer those next challenges. One common thread links all the women interviewed for this book: Whether they were about to sell the company they started for millions or they were working three jobs to make rent, they understood that their vision for the Big Life was utterly their own.

"I never had a path that I wanted to be on. I never knew what the noun was, but I always knew what the adjective was, and that was 'big shot.' I just wanted to be an important person."

"When I started at university as a freshman, I wrote down a life-goals list. It was like, I'm going to law school, and after law school, I'm going to work at the UN. I could see myself as a politician, and I was going to be very worldly."

"I've always had that ambitious drive in me. I had this idea that my career could be something bigger than me. It started as just an idea. I had the vision of what I wanted my career to look like before I was even working. I wanted to make my own stamp."

These women didn't need to be convinced that they could do interesting things with their lives. They weren't bogged down by a quarter-life crisis or confused about what path to follow. They knew nothing was off-limits. They understood that the Big Life doesn't start with a nugget of sage advice from some remote mentor, and that ultimately the journey is much deeper and richer than any path suggested by the guy running the career counseling department at college. The Big Life is about making yourself a stronger, happier person—whatever that means *for you*. These women understood that dreams come in all shapes and sizes, and that there is no one pre-prescribed picture of what the Big Life can look like.

ON YOUR OWN TERMS

You've inherited a world that has moved beyond the idea of "having it all."

Whatever that means.

You want to define success on your own terms. You have no interest in climbing that dusty old corporate ladder, even if it leads to a corner office with a killer view and a collection of Louboutins in a massive closet—that's not what's important to you. You want to forge your own path. You want a career born from your passions. You want validation in the work-place, and a culture that supports and inspires you—whether that means providing opportunities for you to do good in the world or the chance to have a vodka tonic with your col-leagues after a long-ass week. You have a side hustle that you're hoping will turn into the next big thing, and give-back projects that matter to you.

This is a new work-world order. It might seem obvious and expected—after all, most of your friends see the world this way too. But this isn't the way things have always been. The truth is that the game has changed, and *you're* changing it. You are demanding candor and authenticity in everything—especially with salary transparency. And that's starting con-versations about equal pay across the board. When you insist on freedom from the office and fewer face-time meetings, it has bigger implications for all of us. You're actually paving the road now for an easier conversation ahead about how we make room for ambition and children. You're replacing the cold transactional networking previous generations had to suffer through with warm, friendly groups of colleagues who are endlessly devoted to helping one another succeed—in work and in life. The cynicism that was the 20-something trade-mark of your Gen X bosses (we practically invented the eye roll) has been replaced by overwhelming optimism and positivity.

Your Big Life isn't all about work either. No one dreams of working all day and then coming home to some shoebox apartment, tipping cat food into a bowl, and sitting down to eat cold leftover pizza while watching Netflix. The life you imagine for yourself is full in every way. Your Big Life has you running from meetings to lunch to volunteer opportunities to cocktails. You can see yourself traveling too. You want to experience everything. At the end of the week, you meet up with the superhot someone who adores you and talks proudly about your big ambitions to his or her friends.

The key is that you're not waiting for someday. You are living your version of the Big Life now, while acknowledging that it will change and grow as you do.

YOU MIGHT HAVE A CLEAR VISION . . . OR NOT

Maybe you could imagine the course you wanted your Big Life to take early on. Gabriella, 28, has had a major vision for herself since she was a kid growing up in a small New Hampshire town. As a teen, to pay for the private high school that she knew would give her a leg up in the world, she refinished discarded pieces of furniture, turning them into charming vintage treasures that she then sold for a nice profit. In college, she created a business that helped women overseas sell their handmade goods, and now she's started a fintech company focused on young women. If you ask her what her ultimate destination is, Gabriella says without a pause, "Governor." That is clarity. While she's not necessarily going to be taking the oath of office soon—and it's not an easy step from where she is today—being able to name it can help her strategize and develop a rounded outlook on what she'll need to do to eventually step into that role.

But even if you can't imagine the specifics of your Big Life, that doesn't mean the world isn't yours for the taking.

Maybe you can identify with Sarah, 24. She left behind her parents and beloved brothers in rural New York to pursue her Big Life with her sorority sisters in New York City. Sarah's friends are jumping right into dream jobs. One friend has a job as an assistant editor at a major magazine, and another has a gig that's landed her on the red carpet in a fancy dress interviewing celebs. Sarah can't help feeling slightly self-conscious that she still can't name her ultimate goal. Deep down, she knows she could reach any goal she set for herself, if only she knew what *those goals actually were*. So how is a Badass Babe supposed to start building her Big Life when she doesn't even know how to put together the basic pieces?

IT'S ALL ABOUT THE MEANING

Right now, Sarah doesn't know what her dream actually is, so for the moment, she's grinding away at a commission-based job at a real estate company. This job is simply a placeholder, but she knows the *feeling* she's after, and that's what really matters. Sarah wants to fall in love and have a family and go to work every day at a job that makes her feel smart and capable. Ultimately, she knows these pieces will make up a life that's full of meaning for her.

There's so much talk these days about finding your passion or fulfilling your purpose, but that feels like such a high bar, doesn't it? The message the world is sending is that if you can't find your passion or your purpose, then you're lost. But I see things differently. For me, it all starts and ends with the meaning. Ask yourself what means the most to you, and that's where you'll find the core of your Big Life. It's what we all want: to do something meaningful for ourselves, for someone else, and for the world.

It has been my greatest honor to create work that has been meaningful in the lives of young women. My mission is to make you feel smarter, stronger, and, most importantly, validated. It can be incredibly lonely to grow into who you're meant to be. Especially when your vision doesn't fit with the way things have always been done. But what matters most is that you feel empowered to fight for that vision. That's the meaning of my message: Your dreams are worth achieving, and you are worth your dreams.

Your meaning doesn't necessarily have to be weighty and serious. Fun is meaningful; adventure is meaningful. And the beautiful thing about crafting your own Big Life is that meaning can be expressed in any way: running your own tech company, saving a corner of the world at a nonprofit you founded, writing a novel, writing code, raising a family, or running marathons.

THE MEANING IS YOUR NORTH STAR

It's meaning that matters, whether you're the chick who has known what she's wanted to do since sixth grade or you're still trying to piece it all together and stay open to every possibility imaginable. The meaning is your North Star, and if you follow it, you'll go somewhere big.

The Big Life isn't about ticking off a list of goals—or some elusive someday when you've hit a bunch of external life markers. There's no need to wait for the job or the guy to feel supremely satisfied. There's no magical moment when you suddenly sit back and start enjoying it all. You want to enjoy it all starting *now*.

The Escape Hatch

An Escape Hatch is an easy way out of the promise you made to yourself when you were 16 to go for something big. In every sci-fi movie ever, the Escape Hatch is the kind of thing you use to dodge a Big Scary Alien Monster. But the truth is, even when the hero uses it, she ends up fighting that monster anyway.

BEWARE THE ESCAPE HATCH

LET'S BE HONEST: None of this is easy. You're clearing a forest, charting new territory. It's scary and complicated stuff. At the end of one dinner, a Badass Babe quietly admitted that building her Big Life feels so hard that sometimes she's tempted to move back home and reunite with her high-school boyfriend. As cute and sweet as that guy might be, he's just an Escape Hatch from the hard part of her journey. The Escape Hatch is a shortcut to a life that's safer, a path that's well worn, a story in which you already know the ending. An Escape Hatch is an easy way out of the promise you made to yourself when you were 16 to go for something big. When you're facing a particularly rough moment, it's easy to think that your dream, even if—*especially* if—it's just a feeling and not a concrete goal, isn't realistic, or that you didn't want it anyway, or worse, that you won't be able see it through or don't deserve it after all.

Dreams change. There's no need to pretend that you are exactly the same person you were when you first started planning for the Big Life. Experience adds depth and weight to your vision of yourself. Often you'll be charging down the road toward the Big Life and you'll realize there's another big, fun, fulfilling idea you want to pursue—a plan B. But that's not the same as the Escape Hatch, which is a way to opt out of the quest altogether.

So the questions I asked that Badass Babe are the same ones you should ask yourself: "Am I running toward something or away from something? Am I getting closer to the dream, even though I'm momentarily in a dark place, or am I racing toward something safe that I think will make the darkness go away forever?"

In every sci-fi movie ever, the Escape Hatch is the kind of thing used to dodge a Big Scary Alien Monster. But the truth is, even when the hero uses it, she ends up fighting that monster anyway. And even if that Badass Babe decides to move back home and make a life with her high school boy-friend, she's going to have to figure out how to satisfy that feeling of passion and meaning she wants in life. It's hard to do big things, but you owe it to yourself to stay the course, resist the Escape Hatch, and see where this big adventure takes you.

YOUR STORY IS JUST BEGINNING

Right now, it may be hard to see the direction your story will take. It's not a narrative yet; it's a page brimming over with ideas, goals, thoughts, and hopes. But those early stages of your story are where your Big Life begins. It's where the meaning starts to make itself known. The stories we tell matter—whether it's around my dinner table, over coffee with your friends, or just to yourself when you're trying to make sense of the threads of your life.

We're all in this together, sister. I want you to take the reins of your Big Life, so what follows in these pages is both actionable and inspirational. Let go of the anxiety about *when* or *how,* and focus on honoring your ambition, dreaming big, and building the Big Life you know you deserve.

Badass Babes
CONFESS

What the Big Life Means to Me

"What's most important to me, what I really want in this Big Life, is to capital-L *Live*. That's all I've ever really wanted: to see the world, to create, to love, to have experiences, to care for others, and to make a life for myself that I am proud of."

—LUCINDA, 27

"Every day, the hope of attaining the Big Life keeps me moving forward. I am working toward a life of fulfillment, which includes a challenging and engaging career, an income that allows me certain freedoms and luxuries, and a husband who acts as a true partner in all areas of my life: career, family, heath, and adventures. I want children eventually too! Working toward the Big Life, however, often keeps me from appreciating the present. I have to remind myself that the path toward whatever I am reaching for is equally as transformative and important."

—SIMONE, 24

"In my 20s, I worked hard with financial stability in mind: health insurance, a steady paycheck, bills paid. My goal for my 30s is to create the financial freedom to choose work worth doing and relationships worth having, and the ability to walk away if they don't work out. I don't feel like I have my Big Life yet, but I'm working toward it! I'm in a season of life where work is my priority, but it won't always be that way. I have so many other goals I want to accomplish: volunteer, get married, start a family, travel a bit. The best thing I can do to set myself up for success in the future is to work hard now while still nurturing my passion projects and relationships."

—TABBY, 31

"When I was growing up, I dreamed of having the big dream job, the big dream house, and the handsome husband. I wanted to graduate from an Ivy League school, become an investment banker living in Manhattan, and have a beautiful family—that was my dream life. But now, I've achieved almost all of that (still working on the husband part), and I want a *bigger* job, a *bigger* house, and a *bigger* dream. For me, the Big Life constantly gets *bigger*. My ultimate goal is to be an exceptional businesswoman and an exceptional family woman."

—JADE, 24

"I think about the Big Life in two parts: the life I'm living now and the life I want to live 10 to 20 years from now. How can I make the present moment as big and glorious and exciting as I can? And what choices can I make today to set myself up for an even bigger, even more satisfying future?"

—VICTORIA, 23

"We're conditioned to think that 'having it all' means career, husband, family, friends, et cetera. But really, I think the Big Life is what you want it to be. Are you perfectly content working 15-hour days as a CEO and living alone? That's fine! Do you want to get married and have five kids? That's fine too!

"To me, without a doubt, the Big Life means a big career. And hopefully, one day, that means a (much) larger salary and a high-powered role. Even now at this early stage in my career, I really don't want to work 14-hour days and never take a vacation. Having a healthy, fulfilled life off the clock is really important to me too. I want a great job that I genuinely love doing, friends I see regularly, and, hopefully, a relationship with a man who respects my ambition and has passions of his own, and the freedom to travel. I think everything else will figure itself out too."

—KAYLIN, 22

HOW TO HOST YOUR OWN
Badass Babes
DINNER

My Badass Babes dinners have always followed the same formula: fancy frozen pizza (barbecue chicken is my fave), many bottles of rosé, a killer cheese plate, and the Adele station on Pandora. Sure, you can swap pad thai for pizza and margaritas for the wine, but the food is secondary to the conversation around the table. These are the questions I always ask. They move the discussion from dreams to action tips to strategies for dealing with the subtle everyday friction that keeps us a step away from the Big Life. Even if you're not at a dinner party and are asking these questions only to yourself, the goal is to ultimately make the dream a little bit closer.

1   If I could magically solve one problem for you, what would it be?

2   What did you imagine your life would be like when you were 16 years old?

3   What's your idea of the Big Life now?

4   What part of your dream feels out of your control?

5   What's your side hustle or your passion project? What do you do because it feels fun, meaningful, or interesting, and *not* because it pays?

6   Who is your work idol? Who is your icon of where you'd like to be in 5 years? And what is it about that person that you admire?

7   What's the symbol of power or status in your work world?

8 Does your boss think you're "entitled?"

9 How do you think differently about work than your parents did?

10 What does "work-life balance" mean for you right now? What will it look like for you in the future?

11 Is it mutually exclusive to have the big career, the big ambition, be super independent, *and* have the hot partner and the family?

12 Is 30 still a looming deadline for you? What do you feel you must accomplish by the time you're 30? And what will happen if you don't?

13 What do you look for in a partner? How do you know when someone seems right for you and/or when he or she is not?

14 Do you feel as empowered to craft the relationship you want as you are to create the career you want?

15 Do you need a partner to be as driven as you are?

16 Who usually pays on dates? Do you need to have financial equality in your relationship?

17 Do you have the same idea about marriage as your parents do?

18 What worries you now about having kids?

19 Do you think you'll *have to* stop working to have kids?

20 What's the one thing that you wish you knew now about how your Big Life will take shape?

These questions are meant to spark conversation, not guide you toward a right or wrong answer. So many women who've been to my dinners say that they think about their lives and their possibilities differently once they've heard how other women are tackling these Qs. These are not easy questions—I've found that wine helps though!

2

BYE-BYE, CARRIE BRADSHAW

HOW MILLENNIAL CHICKS ARE CHANGING THE MEANING OF SUCCESS

If we're being honest, at one point, your idea of a successful woman probably looked a lot like Carrie Bradshaw in *Sex and the City*. It's a seductive fantasy of sexy work parties, chic new clothes, hot restaurants, and handsome power players. And *pshaw* to the idea of a palatial apartment—who needs it when you have all those gorgeous Manolo Blahniks in the closet. Carrie's life is enviable. She pecks away on her computer between shopping and brunches with friends, and her musings becoming fodder for her very own column. She's in control of her time and also her money, and we all know where most of that goes: shoes.

Or maybe you imagined your first job would look more like Andy Sachs's in *The Devil Wears Prada*. She's full of fierce integrity with a vision that the world will one day recognize her talent. Andy knows in her heart that she has something big to contribute, and she's desperate to make her mark on the world on her own terms (sound familiar?). But first, she has to learn what the world wants from her—which turns out to be getting an ultrahot, 180-degree Starbucks coffee in record time.

But in the end, Andy realizes her true purpose and ditches it all (except the hair and makeup) for a job that speaks to her soul. That's the enduring allure of Andy: We all want to make our work matter—to ourselves and to the world.

These are both amazing fairy tales, but when you look at the reality of your life now, they feel so . . . dated, don't they?

In *Sex and the City,* despite the flashy careers of the main characters, their power is largely reflected by the men they're dating. Mr. Big? I mean, come on! He's about as emotionally supportive as a houseplant. The only thing appealing about him is his car and driver! Who needs that now? You have Uber.

While Andy Sachs's job might be tough at times, it's only one job. How hard is it to fetch coffee and answer a phone? The entry-level assistant job is basically a relic. The job "a million girls would kill for" looks completely different today. Yes, phone calls have to be placed, lunches ordered, and meetings scheduled, but those tasks are shoehorned between other pressing matters. If Andy were an "assistant" at *Runway* now, she'd be posting to social media, filing stories for the website, filming digital videos for the YouTube site, fact-checking senior reporters, following up with corporate on e-commerce initiatives, and building the influencer network.

Listen, you know you can't fast-forward to the part where you are the rock-star CEO or you've closed a big Series A for your kick-ass start-up. And so you see your early gigs of coffee fetching and schedule keeping as the medicine you have to take to get to where you really want to be in the world. But the tricky part is that where you want to be, and the path to get there, could be different from anything anyone's ever done before.

THE NEW WORK-WORLD ORDER

I spent the early part of my journalism career interviewing powerful women about the secrets of their success and their advice to young women. Martha Stewart said, "Don't stab people in the back." Madeleine Albright said, "You have to be extra smart and well prepared . . . women have to try twice as hard." Barbara Walters, my personal role model, gave me a quote that has become a mantra for me: "Don't imagine that your life now is the way it's always going to be. You have no idea the adventures in store for you. You have no idea how interesting your life can become." All *amazing* advice. But these are icons from a different generation, when there was basically one woman at the table and she was a pioneer simply by insisting that everyone move over a little and make room for her to sit down. They challenged the traditional roles carved out for women, and their values represent some level of gratitude at the chance to be heard. That's not your fight. You're at the table. Now you want to customize your role and write new rules that work for you, and if that disrupts the status quo, bring it on! Ultimately, you want *freedom*—from the office, from the entrenched ways of doing things, from the entitlement swipes from your bosses, from the narrow definition of success that puts money or status above happiness.

Take Vanessa, who since college had been slogging through entry-level jobs at rinky-dink beauty start-ups and internships at indie brands (read: cool cache but zero pay) and finally landed a mid-level gig at a *huge* prestige beauty company. Like the magical moment when you meet a man who is hot, successful, *and* available, this job let her marry her passion for design and her need to be well paid. Relax and let it ride, right? WRONG. After a few months of high-fives on every project that came her way, V felt that she was ready to move up a level . . . but rather than go for a promotion, like the one offered to the woman before her and the woman before her, she had the balls to push back *hard* to negotiate a custom title and role that allowed her to span multiple departments in the organization.

It's not as cold-blooded as it sounds. V isn't one of those über-confident chicks who are used to marching into a boss's office and demanding anything, let alone something as important and emotionally complex as a promotion. She's not the girl who rates herself off the charts on every performance review and thinks she deserves special treatment. Entitlement is not her M.O. This is a woman who felt every one of those nagging doubts about who she should be and where she should go as she navigated her postcollege career path. Every move in her personal life and her professional life was carefully weighed, thought-out, and considered. So, where did she get the guts to ask for special treatment? It's my life, she reasoned. I only get one. And it has to be good.

Vanessa is still operating within the big-company ecosystem. But Allison is one of those women who saw the corporate life laid out ahead of her and said thanks, but no thanks. She got "downsized" in 2008, and rather than look for a similar gig, she decided to teach herself how to code—after all, it was the developers who were largely untouched when big corporations started to thin their ranks as profits declined. Coding put her more in control of her destiny. In fact, she launched a business to teach other women how to code, so they could be in control of their careers too. It's a movement, but Allison doesn't see herself as a revolutionary—she was focused on only one step at a time. However, she'd eventually wandered so far off the beaten path that she'd cleared the way for a whole army of young women with dreams of being in control of their own destinies. "You'd still have to tell me I'm changing the world," Allison demurs. "That's not how I think about it."

So, how did an entire generation of young women suddenly step off the ladder and feel empowered to carve their own damn paths?

TIPS FROM CHICKS AT THE TABLE

HOW VANESSA CUSTOMIZED HER ROLE AND GOT THE PROMOTION SHE REALLY WANTED

"I waited until my yearly review with my manager and came armed with a list of successes I'd had and ready to talk about my vision for how I saw my position evolving. I took notes while we talked and turned them into a proper memo, making the argument that my vision for the job would actually help modernize the structure of the department and be a model for other teams. I knew that my boss would send the memo to his boss, and I made sure it was as thorough and professional as possible. It took many more months than I expected to get the plan approved, and by the time I got my new role, I had an even broader vision of myself. The whole process taught me that if the company didn't want to support me, I'd find a role that suited me better elsewhere. I'm happy with my new position, but now I have my eye on my next move."

ENTER THE RECESSION [STAGE LEFT]

Your world can basically be divided into before the recession and after the recession. Flashback to 2007, when the fixation on outward and obvious signs of wealth were everywhere! On *Gossip Girl*, the sweet, sultry voice of Kristen Bell "XOXO, Gossip Girl" took you into a world of delicious drama couched in unbelievable luxury. Every paparazzi shot of Jessica Simpson featured three things: her big bright smile, a small Maltipoo dog named Daisy, and a lust-inducing Louis Vuitton Takashi Murakami handbag dangling beautifully off one arm.

Everyone wanted that bag. But today, it's easier to see Jessica's go-to bag for what it really is: a way-overpriced $2,500-plus handbag with crazy cartoon characters on it. Oh, It Bag lust . . . where did you go?

Before the recession, such luxuries weren't necessarily out of the question. In the 1990s and early 2000s, things were seriously looking up for your typical American family. The economy was prospering big-time—jobs were being added to the workforce, stocks were quadrupling or better, and the median income grew by 10 percent! Hello new SUV/swimming pool/family vacation. With all that abundance, it's *almost* understandable that putting yourself on a yearlong waiting list for a cherry-dotted Louis Vuitton bag sounded like a semi-reasonable idea.

This was the cultural backdrop of the world when I became the editor-in-chief of *Seventeen* in 2007. The economy was booming and the spoils of affluence seemed within reach, so why worry about having a powerful career when it didn't seem like it would be a problem to attain one? It wasn't that girls didn't have big dreams for themselves. But it was as if they'd just *assumed* they'd be successful. For years, I had been running a girls' leadership campaign at another teen magazine, but by 2007, getting girls interested in leadership was like forcing yourself to go for a handful of raw baby carrots when you'd been hungrily eyeing a bag of Doritos. No thanks! Leadership sounded like *work*. Being a leader sounded like you'd be the shrill girl with no friends sitting at the front of the class with her hand in the air always trying to get the teacher to call on her. The female role models of leadership in politics at that time—like Madeleine Albright and Condoleezza Rice—felt a little dusty and unrelatable. Groundbreaking female CEO powerhouses like Meg Whitman, who was then at eBay, and Indra Nooyi at PepsiCo didn't have the kind of jobs that felt sexy and cool (not when girls like Lauren Conrad were doing glossy magazine internships by day and drinking champagne at Les Deux by night).

In the years right before the recession, the message girls were sending was "Don't push me." Received. So I positioned the content at *Seventeen* to reflect this reality. "It's FUN to be Seventeen" was the new tagline. We focused on fashion, beauty, boys, and, yes, fun. Blake Lively wore Chanel on the cover. Miley Cyrus wore Marc Jacobs. Beyoncé was dripping in black diamonds. Shopping? Oh yes! Confidence? Amen! Give back? Absolutely—we have more than enough! Leadership or career? Meh. Don't push me.

But the recession changed everything. Suddenly, success wasn't a given. There was a new awareness about money (or lack thereof). The fantasy of getting an LV for your sweet 16 or a shiny new SUV as a graduation gift was over. Not even college was a sure thing. If your older sister was thinking about changing her major again and staying in college for a total of 5 or 6 years, forget it. You knew you were going to need to finish in 4. Maybe 3.

And so young women, right on the verge of coming into their own, became mobilized. They were determined to take control of their destiny. They wanted internships in high school, they started businesses in college, and they voraciously sought out women in power to learn their secrets to success. Rather than wait for jobs that didn't exist, take a gig at a coffee shop, or hit up struggling parents for financial support, a whole new generation of smart young women took their destiny into their own hands—literally. For this generation, social media became the hammer of their power, and they have been wielding it since they got their first iPhones. Suddenly, access to the biggest celebs, the most powerful politicians, and even Oprah was only a tweet away! Young women were branding themselves on Instagram, launching businesses on Etsy, and becoming YouTube mega-stars. The disruption in my corner of the world was obvious: Fashion editors who had spent their entire careers inching closer to the front row suddenly lost their seats to bloggers like Tavi Gevinson, who was all of 13 in 2009 when she sat front and center during Rodarte's Fashion Week show, and Leandra Medine, who was 20 when she launched her megapopular blog Man Repeller. Forget the *Today* show; theSkimm, founded in 2012 by two NBC interns, began as an email digest of the biggest headlines of the day and revolutionized the way we get the news. So long snooty department store makeup counters; Birchbox, a subscription beauty service founded by Hayley Barna and Katia Beauchamp, who met in business school in 2010, changed the way we experience new beauty products. These young women jumped out of the frying pan and into the fire to burn down old ideas of how business should work and what women in business should be like.

I mean, you know. You were there.

And so was Jordan, who was finishing up her degree at Harvard Business School in 2009. You can't help being impressed from the first minute you meet this Glamazon beauty, 6 feet tall in bare feet, with a sexy mane of perfectly messy black waves. She has presence with a capital *P*. And then you get to her résumé. A few years out of business school, she founded her first company to disrupt the supply chain in a stagnant consumer-goods industry, became managing director of a program that shows people how to leverage their tech skills and passions to find the perfect job, and was a resident at a big-wig incubator and a mentor for several enviable start-ups. Plus, in her free time, Jordan sings lead vocals in a band, climbs mountains, and runs marathons. Oh, and now she runs a very high-profile organization whose zeitgeist-y mission is to inspire girls to go into computer science. NBD.

Jordan wasn't born into a family of entrepreneurs or risk-takers. It was necessity that put her on her twisty path. She grew up in a blue-collar town and was raised by her grandfather, who was the first in his family to move from farming to industrial work. To make the point that leadership wasn't part of the family dinner conversation, she tells the story that when her grandad was offered a promotion to foreman, he turned it down because he didn't want to boss his friends around. "That's my family," she said. "Trust in God, but don't take a promotion."

For Jordan, though, it was the national economic earthquake that solidified her passion to create her own destiny. "A lot of people who played by the rules got screwed over in 2008—they got laid off anyway. I have friends who killed it in law school and had offers at blue-chip firms that no longer existed by the time they graduated. I had friends in business school who were being sponsored by Lehman Brothers, and one semester into school they were told, 'Sorry, we're not paying for you anymore . . . *because we don't exist.*'" And so, what's an ambitious girl to do? "There became this understanding that just because you play by the rules doesn't mean you're going to get ahead. The only way to make sure you do is to pick yourself, whether that means creating a company so you get to hire yourself to be CEO, which is what I did, or taking a huge risk on a huge risk and hoping it pays off. And hoping you're smart enough and strong enough that if it doesn't, you can pick yourself up and start again."

So basically, you were faced with a choice to believe in a system that was suddenly broken or to believe in yourself. A whole new generation of young women chose disruption over the status quo and community over competition.

CHANGE THE GAME TO BE THE WAY YOU WANT IT

You get it. Your industry has been going about things the same way for a long, long . . . *long* time. And sure, it works fine. But to you, a steady ship is a solid base for building exciting new opportunities—and you're dying to dig in. You have a fresh approach to tackling old ideas and can't help wondering what would happen if things were done *your* way. You're a disrupter.

HOW TWO FRIENDS FROM GRAD SCHOOL UPENDED THE FASHION INDUSTRY

Jennifer Hyman and Jenny Fleiss have a closet that puts Carrie Bradshaw's to shame. But the thing about these fancy frocks is that they're rented, and instead of simply wearing the dresses, they founded a whole company based on them: Rent the Runway. On a semester break from her MBA program, Jenn told her friend Jenny about her idea to "democratize the luxury industry." Screw the old idea of the haves and the have-nots—particularly during a crushing recession that's reset the entire idea of how we spend money. Why shouldn't all women have pretty dresses *on demand*?

Jenn also knew that the way to reach her generation was by giving them what they want—*experiences*. She spent a short but meaningful stint at Starwood Hotels, where she learned that some "industries that are chaotic are ripe for innovation." Her idea to shake up the travel industry? The first-ever travel wedding registry. Why register for fine china when you can have a trip to Beijing instead? She cofounded Rent the Runway on the same principle—experience over ownership. And to get back to that dress you want to rent: While it's obviously great that you can show up to an event tonight in a $750 Badgley Mischka dress by dropping only $80, Jenn wants you to know that she's a "disrupter," and not in the business of simply "renting frilly dresses."

"I think the tech and business community have a stereotype that because we are young women who happen to like wearing dresses, we started the company because we love shopping or because we are obsessed with fashion," she told *Fortune* magazine. "We saw a movement toward collaborative consumption across all sectors of the economy, and we started Rent the Runway because we wanted to change and democratize one of the biggest industries in the world." Damn.

SISTERHOOD FOR THE WIN

When you're hit with a great idea, you don't stay up all night drinking coffee alone, frantically sketching out plans, and plotting how you'll get from point A to point B. You're the kind of chick who wants to share her ideas. You know your bestie will have great input about design, and you've always wanted to team up with that marketing-expert chick you like so much from your coworking space. Your ideas are big, but your heart—and your desire to bring together talented people to create something amazing—is even bigger. You're a collaborator.

HOW SISTERHOOD TURNED A GIRLY OBSESSION INTO A MASSIVE EMPIRE

Every women's magazine keeps a huge beauty closet behind locked doors. It's filled with every product imaginable for hair, skin, and nails. After a long week, I've been known to take home bags brimming with hair masks, face masks, mani kits, and glittery lip glosses. Each item will soothe, buff, gloss, or smooth you into a more perfect, happier version of yourself. It's the same deliciously reassuring feeling you get walking down the aisles in Sephora. The promise of pretty is so alluring. And it's also pretty *powerful*.

The world has put up a giant wall between the kinds of things that women obsess over and real power.

It would be easy to write off a love of beauty products as a silly distraction—after all, it seems like the rest of the world has put up a giant wall between the kinds of things that women obsess over and real power. But I dare you to tell Michelle Phan that her $100 million empire doesn't give her a very strong platform to stand on and have an impact on the world. Actually, I bet Michelle doesn't care who does or doesn't think she's powerful—she's had First Lady Michelle Obama on speed dial ever since they toured Asia together as part of a Malala-inspired "Let Girls Learn" campaign. Insert power-fist emojis here.

Your first experience with Michelle Phan starts like this:

"Hi, gorgeous."

Or maybe . . .

"Hello, majestic one."

When you hear Michelle's velvety voice and see that warm smile pop up on your phone in one of her tutorials, you can't help feeling you're meeting a friend who is happy to see you (and who thinks you look great). Her wildly popular YouTube channel features tutorials on everything from "Lunar New Year's Beauty" to "how to make an illuminated floating cloud for your bedroom." Phan effortlessly transforms her own face from naturally pretty to A-list–celebrity polished in mere minutes, and then can create a ridiculously adorable new iPhone case by slapping on a few carefully selected stickers. She's the best friend every girl wants—friendly, warm, and awesome at applying makeup and putting together cute things for your home made out of random bits, aluminum foil, and cotton balls.

You probably already know that Michelle Phan has a classic rags-to-riches tale. When this 20-something waitress was turned down for a job at a department store beauty counter because of her lack of experience, she found a totally new way into the beauty scene. She connected with her audience authentically, in her own bedroom, where she made her first YouTube makeup tutorial on a borrowed laptop. Ten intense years later (she admits she's never off the clock and gets about 4 to 5 hours of sleep per night), this self-made beauty millionaire has turned a girly obsession into a multiplatform empire, including 10 million YouTube subscribers, a beauty-box subscription business, multiple live conferences, and even a record label.

Michelle's real power is how deeply connected she is to her community: "I'm motivated by my love to share and teach. I love sharing things that inspire me, and I love connecting with people. Being part of a community is in the millennial DNA." For Michelle, her community isn't just her zillions of fans and followers; it's other vloggers too. Instead of seeing other young women who are trying to make it big in the beauty space as competition, she sees them as collaborators. Case in point: Phan created Generation Beauty, a conference that brings together the top online beauty, fashion, and life-style gurus for a couple of days of inspiration, fun, and, of course, collecting beauty samples. Another massive piece of Michelle's empire is her subscription beauty biz, ipsy. Yes, it's another way for Michelle to reach her fans, but she also embraces collaboration to the max and shares the spotlight with an amazingly diverse team of vloggers known as the ipsy stylists. Maybe you're into Jaleesa Moses and her old-school Hollywood glam. Or, maybe you click with Christen Dominique, who embraces the power of makeup but encourages women to feel beautiful without it. Want experimental and quirky? Karen O is the ipsy stylist for you.

Michelle's influence is felt beyond the beauty world. She has paved the way for thousands of other young women to see the power of their own expertise, whether it's applying eyeliner, baking pies, or designing jewelry, as a serious *business* opportunity.

THE BIG LIFE HUMBLEBRAG

With new ways to value success come new ways to show it off. These outward symbols have shifted from a flashy show of money to a more meaningful emphasis on experience and freedom. The *Sex and the City*-era Manolos have been replaced as a status symbol by the MacBook Air. It's proof that you are so talented that you can plug in and work from your apartment, in between SoulCycle classes, at Coachella—anywhere. The type of retro velvet-rope parties that *The Devil Wears Prada*-era girls clamored to get into have been replaced by power networking at Cannes Lions, SXSW, Summit at Sea, and the Aspen Ideas Festival. The cushy corner office is a relic, and the real get is a spot at a cool coworking space like WeWork. (Sign of the revolution: WeWork, at 5 years old and with a business model of making you feel like you're working at a tech incubator, is currently valued at $10 billion.)

And in a surprise twist, that early dot-com idea of flat hierarchy and no titles has disappeared, and now young women are negotiating hard for the highest title they can grab. The "office manager" has become the "head of operations;" "HR manager" has become "vice president of human capital and culture;" and "consumer marketing" has become "audience development and monetization strategy." Today's title brag makes Patrick Bateman's 1980-era business-card one-upmanship in *American Psycho* seem like such a petty power play. After all, the bigger the title, the more recruiters who will find you on LinkedIn!

THE BIG GLITTERING OASIS

I know you can get your hands on a MacBook Air . . . and you've probably already negotiated an amazingly kick-ass title. Congratulations.

But chances are, you're not likely to find yourself power-networking at Summit Series or seated next to Arianna Huffington at her dinner at the Aspen Ideas Festival to discuss "developing a sense of wonder."

I'm not saying it's not in your future, but the truth is, it's not in the cards for most people. It can be so easy to obsess over the Instagram photos of the select few who somehow do get to SXSW, acting all casual and writing ironic captions as they wait in a long line at the Thai-Southern fusion food truck. The FOMO can be totally consuming. How can it not when you're seeing posts from chicks who are hanging out at rooftop parties featuring aerialists? Or at the zombie-apocalypse-inspired BuzzFeed party where scary, face-painted bartenders serve brain-themed cocktails? It just. Never. Ends.

By the way, those were real parties. I did not make those up. And FWIW, I wasn't there either.

I'm not going to tell you to get over it . . . or that it doesn't matter.

It *does* matter, but not in the way you might think. It's sort of a natural first response to say, "Why does she have that ONE THING I want, and I don't?" The thing is, you wouldn't really want it if it wasn't the kind of thing people bragged about having. It's not exclusive if everyone has it.

It's worth remembering that even the people who are at those parties can't keep away from their Instagram feeds—

they're looking at pics from other parties and wondering why they weren't invited.

The FOMO still happens to me. I'll find myself face-to-face with someone who actually takes gleeful pride in telling me about some event that I wasn't invited to—or that I haven't heard of. I feel dumb and experience 45 seconds of gut-wrenching awfulness. Then I remember when I interviewed Vera Wang, who built a fashion empire that catapulted her personal fortune to more than $400 million. She said that she deals with disappointment by *wallowing* in it. And this is a woman who famously lost her shot to be the editor-in-chief of *Vogue* to one of her colleagues, a young Anna Wintour. Cue wallowing.

So, I acknowledge that it was that person's small victory to make me feel like crap and feel whatever I need to feel for a minute. Maybe two. Then I'm over it. I'm not a big fan of who-is-up and who-is-down kind of power. Thankfully, you live in the age of collaboration, when, as Michelle Phan said, everyone you want to be around is trying to help everyone else get more power too!

And let's face it: When you read some woman's post about getting a massive promotion, getting engaged, or even running a triathlon, that FOMO quickly morphs into a feeling that you're not kicking ass hard enough. And that if you were doing more, working longer hours, or sleeping less, or were just more amazing, you'd be posting about promotions and marathons too. The feeling isn't motivating; it's paralyzing!

Elizabeth opens up over pizza and rosé at one of my Badass Babes dinners. She's the ultimate hustler, a girl who moved to NYC from the Southwest to follow her dream on her own dime. She has a good gig at a new tech start-up, Tinder dates galore, a share house at the beach in the Hamptons, and she recently traveled to Australia. But all that awesomeness doesn't manage to keep the FOMO at bay. "I look at Instagram, and I look at these girls, and I think, I want to live *your* life," she says. At the same dinner, Kaylin, who had landed a job covering celebs at a major magazine, says all her anxiety about not being awesome enough relates to her career: "I stress about my career constantly. I'm an editorial assistant, and there are people my age who are associate editors, and it freaks me out. Like I'm not moving fast enough; I'm not at a high enough position."

Here's the thing: There will always be someone with a bigger job or a more glamorous vacation or working at a hotter nonprofit that is saving the world (not to mention, we all know those shiny Instagram posts rarely reflect reality—*please*). And so the world turns.

But the big question is this: What does it mean to you? Whether you're fantasizing about being invited to the ultra-exclusive Summit at Sea, being recognized for your hard work with a promotion and a big title, having a romantic vacay on the Amalfi Coast, or even living in Carrie Bradshaw's version of Manhattan, you need to know that a big glittering oasis isn't a place. It's the moment when you feel like you *deserve* all those spoils—whatever those lust-worthy things are that would make you feel special, respected, and loved. You have kicked ass hard enough, and you know that when you walk into a room, you won't feel like you're faking it. You will walk into the room and *own* it. And that's when even more doors open for you.

Know that I don't think having a more tricked-out life on social media is the solution either. You're doing something cool? By all means, share, but don't think that posting a pic of your amazing weekend running a half-marathon followed by making homemade ravioli with organic kale you grew on your fire escape is going to squash that pesky feeling that parts of your life aren't awesome enough.

It's hard to do big things, and you have to give yourself credit for every victory, big and small. Yeah, it might be impossible to feel like you're crushing it when you're doing crappy tasks for your boss while other chicks are meeting with investors and giving talks at SXSW—but the next time you're standing in line waiting for your boss's chai latte, borrow this mantra: Your life now isn't the way it's always going to be. You have no idea the adventures in store for you, and you have no idea how interesting your life can become.

THE BIG LIFE
CONVERSATION

GABI GREGG
Fashion blogger, designer, and
founder of Gabifresh.com

HOW A BODY-POSITIVE BLOGGER BUILT HER OWN BRAND ON HER OWN TERMS

One of the original plus-size body-positive bloggers, Gabi Gregg (a.k.a. Gabi Fresh) broke new territory in celebrating her shape and her style sense. She was the first "Twitter jockey" at MTV, wrote a column for me at *Seventeen,* and had a regular gig at *InStyle*. She has helped curvy young women own their place in the fashion world, and now she's helping to dress them! She has had huge success as a designer for Swimsuits for All and plans to launch her own line.

Ann: What did you imagine your life would be like when you were 16?

Gabi: I was interested in creative fields, but I was so lost because I didn't know what that looked like. I came from a family full of teachers, but I didn't have a good idea of what else existed besides becoming like a teacher, lawyer, or doctor. I knew I loved fashion, and I remember thinking I wanted to work for Anna Wintour because she was the only real figurehead that I knew about in the fashion world.

A: It must have been tough growing up in Detroit in the 2000s as the automotive industry collapsed. Did the economic crisis in this country affect the possibilities you saw for yourself?

G: Yes! Especially when the recession hit. I graduated with a degree in international relations and African American studies from Mount Holyoke College in 2008—it was the worst time ever to enter a new career and find an entry-level job. I couldn't find *anything*. I moved home and applied to local restaurants as a waitress or a hostess. I applied to law firms as a legal aid. I applied to a few temp agencies. I couldn't even get a job at Starbucks, so it was a disheartening time.

Still, I wanted to work in fashion. So, I focused on my blog—I thought it would be a good way to show my writing style and fashion sense. I thought it was better than being unemployed and having nothing to say for myself.

A: It's smart advice for anyone just starting out to create something of their own to show what they can do. But this wasn't your side gig—you needed to earn money to support yourself while building this venture. How did you do it?

G: In the beginning, I would get free clothes [from designers], but I was scared to turn it into something that was 100 percent monetized, because I thought I would be a sell-out.

37

In the beginning years of bloggers, brands were still very slowly trickling into the idea of working with us in a big way and giving us the money we deserved, so even though I had a few offers here and there, it wasn't something I could totally live off of.

I was able to use my social media expertise to get a yearlong gig at MTV—I was their first Twitter jockey. In that year, I was able to continue my blog, and when I left MTV, I decided that I wanted to be in the fashion industry—on my own terms. I gave myself 1 year to see if I could make it happen. I thought as long as I can pay my rent without any assistance from my parents, then I could make this work. I would figure out the rest. I ate ramen. I got an apartment with a Craigslist roommate and slept on the floor under a faux-fur coat.

My friends would always make fun of me because, at the time, I had a certain amount of success: I was a personality at MTV, I had quotes in the *New York Times*, I was on *Good Morning America* . . . but I could barely afford to, like, eat.

A: You were insta-famous, but you were broke. How did you turn your blog into a moneymaking business?

G: Most of my money back then came from Google ads, and once in a while, I would get a sponsored post here and there. But my fee wasn't superhigh. After a few months, I was tapped by Eloquii, a plus-size brand, to be their brand ambassador. It was my first big deal. The check was, like, $20,000, and I was so excited because I'd never seen a figure like that on one check in my life!

Through that deal, I was signed to my management company, and that changed my trajectory. They convinced me to double down on valuing myself and made sure I was charging the right amount. And so I started to get more consistent work. Even with their help, it took me another year to start making money comfortably.

A: Why did you decide to do it on your own rather than capitalize on your success and go work for someone else?

G: To be very frank, I didn't enjoy working at MTV, and that helped me realize that I wanted to work for myself. I didn't love the feeling of being in an office day in and day out. More importantly, I didn't like the feeling of not having control over my image or my voice.

My face was attached to my words at MTV, but I wasn't in control of the message. I didn't like the feeling of having to create blog posts about things I wasn't passionate about. So even though the job was cool from the outside, internally, I was not happy. And that's when I decided that if I'm going to do something that I'm happy with, I have to be in charge of it.

A: Is there someone you model your career after or someone you look at and say, I'd like to have a business like she has?

G: I'm inspired by Beyoncé and people like her who have been in control of their brands and their images. One of the biggest lessons I've learned is that some people aren't going to like you. I'm sure some people think Beyoncé is a bitch, because she wants what she knows is best for her and her brand. I'm inspired by the work ethic and values that certain celebrities stick to in order to make their visions come to life, as opposed to constantly compromising and doing things they don't want to do.

A: Blogging or being an influencer wasn't even a real job a couple of years ago. Is it freeing to forge your own path, or is it terrifying that you're making it up as you go along?

G: I think it's a little bit of both. I love the idea of doing what I want and not letting anyone else determine my path. I've been really good about not comparing myself to other people when it comes to success. I've been really good about not listening to every single voice that told me *not* to quit MTV. My entire life, all the adults and my peers literally thought I was crazy. They were like, "What are you doing? Go get a job!" And I was like, this is going to work out. I had this blind faith. And I was like, if it doesn't work out, that's fine. But I knew I was young enough to at least try.

A: What would you have done if it didn't work?

G: I would have gone and gotten a job. It was hard to get a job right out of college anyway, but I knew that another year of trying wasn't going to make or break my ability to eventually work in corporate America or go to law school if that's what I chose to do. But I didn't want to jump into a career or into law school and hate it. And that's what a lot of my friends did, to be totally honest. They were doing something because they felt like they *had* to. And I was like, I'm 22 years old. I am not going to sign up for a life that I don't want to live just because other people are telling me that's what I should do.

A: You paved the way for other young women to see their own social media power and their own brands as a real career path. What's the one thing you want young influencers to know about the business?

G: The most important thing is knowing what you stand for and what your message is. I always had a clear vision of what I wanted to do: Show people you can be stylish at any size. The whole fashion industry has mostly ignored plus-size women, and if they did talk about plus-size women, it was always about what *not* to wear and how to look thinner. I totally rejected that. I'm not going to be wearing black V-neck A-line dresses for the rest of my life. I love having fun with fashion and experimenting. And so I wanted to bring that message to a larger world.

For me, it's not making the quick check. I think that, especially when you're young, it's so enticing and so tempting to just be like, oh, this company is offering me so much money. But what do you stand for that's larger than that? What do you want your larger message to be? What is your brand about? Is it just about looking cute? What is behind your brand? And I think that's so important because that can help—whether you know your destination or not—to lead your way.

I think we are bringing something else to the table with messaging and in terms of our voices being unique. That's when you can take your brand to the next level and make a difference in the culture.

3

GET A JOB, ANY JOB

EVERYTHING YOU NEED TO KNOW ABOUT SURVIVING IN THE WORKPLACE

Sometimes, when you're having a major philosophical discussion about the Big Life and how you're going to find meaning, passion, respect, and fulfillment, you want someone to tell you exactly what to do. Enough with the endless possibilities and twists and turns; you want some hard-and-fast rules for getting ahead so you can simply keep putting one foot in front of the other. Here they are.

But one caveat: This is probably not the advice that well-respected, well-researched career sites like Levo League, the Muse, *Fortune,* and *Inc.* would give. I don't have statistics or long-term studies to back up my findings. This is advice culled from my own career—I have moved up and around in an industry that's notoriously tricky to navigate. I have hired and occasionally fired employees. I know what makes someone stand out from the crowd and who's hiding from being noticed at all. I have interviewed some of the most powerful women in business—and worked closely with some of them too. I've listened to senior women tell stories about their own paths. And I've been honored to hear hundreds of young women share what has worked for them and what hasn't. And so, with the benefit of my own experience and perspective, I offer some of the lessons I learned that can help you craft your own kick-ass career, no matter what your field.

STEP ONE:
GET A JOB, ANY JOB

In college, I studied English lit and creative writing. I had considered becoming a novelist, but by graduation, that seemed like it would be a recipe for loneliness and financial ruin. So, I thought magazine journalism might be a good place to get started. I sent résumés to all the big magazines—*People, Elle, Cosmopolitan, Newsweek.* I had a few informational interviews (which, by the way, are totally worth doing so you get practice and they get to know you) but zero job offers. I still have a stack of the rejection letters—including one from *Seventeen*!

When I graduated from college in the mid-1990s, the country was in the middle of a major recession, but despite the lack of jobs, I had rent to pay! My Filofax (now a relic) was full of notes about people to get in touch with, places to research for my cover letters, and ideas about where I could

THE BEST COVER LETTER ADVICE I'VE EVER GOTTEN— THAT I'M PASSING DOWN TO YOU!

When I was an intern at *Rolling Stone* during the semester before I graduated college, I made an appointment with one of the senior editors to get his job-search advice. Skip the HR department, he said, and write a letter directly to an editor or an executive editor. (It might be the president of the company where you want to work or the head of the department where you see yourself ending up.) Don't write a fan letter. Don't say how much you've always wanted to work there. Write in as much detail as possible about why that company appeals to you and what you have to offer them. This is an opportunity to tell someone how your POV on the world can benefit her business. And this is your opportunity to make your résumé pop out of a giant pile of résumés with similar experience but none of the same heart!

look for a job. I was *hustling*. Every week, I'd go to the career services center at New York University and look through a giant dusty binder of job listings. (Listen, it was the '90s. The Internet was about 5 minutes old, and there was no Indeed app to scrape all the job sites for me!)

It was while poring through that binder that I saw a listing for an executive assistant position at the *American Lawyer* magazine. If this doesn't sound like a Dream Job, it's because it isn't—or it certainly wasn't mine. But it was a job. At a magazine. That paid. I wore the worst suit that has ever been designed, made three copies of my résumé as career services instructed, and took the train uptown to the *American Lawyer* offices. But this time, during the interview, instead of the glazed eyes of a human resources drone whose job was to turn away 99 percent of candidates, I was met by a woman tasked with finding her own replacement, and I actually saw a spark of interest. I seized on that flicker of possibility and became determined to keep talking until it was clear that she had decided to hire me. She offered me the job the next day.

While a job at the *American Lawyer* wasn't the glossy glam-magazine job I'd dreamed about, it was the job I *could get*. And though I had a flicker of an idea about what direction I wanted my career to take, it ultimately didn't matter that much. Whether you have honed in on your Dream Job with laserlike focus or have no idea what career you want, know that just getting *a job* is better than flopping about trying to figure out the right path while burning through any savings left in your bank account. When you're a total newbie, you have little more to offer than your ability to be on time, answer the phones professionally, and not screw up (although I did that too!). You are there to learn the rules of work. Why the receptionist is your secret weapon for office intel and lunch orders that get delivered on time. How to schedule appointments with the busiest people in the world. Which time-wasting, desk-lurking people to avoid. How to send emails that are polite, to the point, *and* get answered in a timely fashion. Why you should never send an email that you wouldn't want forwarded to your boss. How to figure out whether the dude in the cubicle next to you is about to ask you out and how to duck the invite so things don't get weird. And, ultimately, how to make your boss love you and move you into bigger and better roles. You will learn these things no matter where you work, so don't stress about the Dream Job.

At first, my job at the *American Lawyer* was to answer phones, order lunch, and distribute memos. I quickly moved into the role of fact-checker, in which I basically re-reported the writer's stories and made sure all the ampersands and commas of the law firms' names were in the right places. Are you still awake? Working at the *American Lawyer* actually turned out to be a *phenomenal* opportunity. The boss, Steven Brill, is a brilliant, legendary journalist who chomped cigars, yelled at reporters (including me), and also had a new vision for a media company. In addition to running the *American Lawyer,* he launched Court TV, owned a collection of newspapers, and created a digital platform for attorneys. I didn't realize it at the time, but I was learning how to create multiplatform media, which later would shape my own vision for my role in the industry. Some of the most respected journalists in the country had been in Brill's newsroom: Pulitzer Prize–winning journalist James B. Stewart; Jill

Abramson, who became the first female executive editor of the *New York Times*, and financial journo bulldog James Cramer, who famously said that Brill bit him on the ear in the heat of an argument! I used to see Dan Abrams, now chief legal affairs anchor for ABC News, in heavy makeup on his way to the Court TV studio. And when I met the *Today* show's Natalie Morales, who was also on Court TV, we realized that we'd probably bumped into each other in the office kitchen.

A week after I started my job, O. J. Simpson took his infamous ride down the California highway in his white Bronco. We all huddled around a small TV in the conference room to watch the drama unfold. Suddenly, courtroom journalism wasn't so snoozy after all!

AIM FOR YOUR DREAM JOB, BUT FYI, ANY JOB WILL DO

❶ If you know what your Dream Job is, apply for it! What do you have to lose? But don't worry if you don't get it yet. Take any job in your field that will give you the chance to learn how an office works and some of the basics of your industry.

❷ If you don't know what your Dream Job looks like, apply for gigs at organizations that appeal to you. Toss your hat in the ring for positions that sound fun and interesting, even if you're not sure that's where you see yourself ending up. You never know what kind of job is going to light a spark!

❸ Look for big-picture themes from your job that you can use in your next job interview. Are you on the front lines of a reorganization? Is your team innovating new processes or products? Is there a rich history at your company that you're proud to be a part of?

❹ Don't screw up.

47

You've research the company, Googled the boss, connected with the HR department on LinkedIn, checked out the Glassdoor reviews, and written a killer cover letter—and finally you got a callback! Don't panic, sister. You got this!

SIT AT THE EDGE OF YOUR SEAT

You have to earn the right to sit back in your chair—and if you're going for your first job or second (or even third), you haven't. You have to lean forward and show respect to your interviewer. Under no circumstances should you bring coffee or a water bottle into an interview and put it on the interviewer's desk. Automatic disqualification!

BE ENGAGING

It's your job to make the interview a conversation. Don't make your interviewer work to figure out what's so great about you. Come prepared to tell her what makes you so good for the job and what she doesn't already know about you from your résumé. She wants to know specifically why you want to work for her. You should ask questions too, but never about money (until later) and never about anything that you could find out in your research. I'm a huge fan of questions that connect you to the work the company is doing, let the boss know you've done your background checks, and flatter the interviewer just a smidge, like this: "I loved that campaign you launched last fall. I did a similar program for the nonprofit I work with. What was your favorite part of that campaign?"

WRITE A THANK-YOU NOTE

I used to be a stickler about handwritten thank-you notes. And if you're going that route, get classic flat note cards with your name or initials engraved on them. No foldover cards. No flowers or butterflies. Simple and sophisticated. That said, I've softened my stance on the handwritten note and think it's fine to email a thank-you. In fact, if you know the clock is ticking toward a decision or it's a digital job, email is the first line of defense. The crucial point, though, is that your thank-you has to specifically mention something you talked about in your meeting, and it has to be thoughtful—and short. Five sentences MAX. Or it's TL;DR. Simply thanking your interviewer for her time is a waste of her time. You have to say something that makes you stand out from the crowd. The most nerve-racking part of the proper follow-up protocol is how to follow up again if you don't hear back. The truth is that people are phenomenally busy and email can easily get lost in the shuffle. If you don't hear back in 2 weeks, email again reiterating how excited you'd be to join an organization that's doing such amazing things. If you still don't hear back, some people say a third email another 2 weeks later is okay. I think it's just like a dude who doesn't return your text or your smiley face reminder: He's moved on and so should you.

STEP TWO:
LISTEN TO EVERYTHING

When I finally moved out of fact-checking purgatory and into a proper reporter role at the *American Lawyer*, I sat in a big open "pit" of more-senior reporters, and by listening to the conversations around me, I learned how to be a reporter too.

On my one side was a shy, sort-of-nerdy guy who used to answer the phone in a surprisingly commanding voice, "Vin Diesel here!" (Not his real name, but you get the point!) When he knew he was closing in on some juicy bit of info, he would start to boss around his sources in a really aggressive, challenging kind of way. So I tried that too. Um, not the approach for me. I couldn't keep up that level of bravado. The reporter on my other side pretended he was sort of clueless so that people would explain really complex ideas in easy ways. It felt weird for me to play into a stereotype that most of the male lawyers I was reporting on already held about me. So I kept listening, and I eventually picked up bits and pieces that felt right for me—friendly, well-researched, a smidge pushy.

TIPS FROM CHICKS AT THE TABLE

HOW PIPER *LITERALLY* LISTENED IN

"My first job as an assistant was working for a legendary filmmaker. Part of my job was being on her conference calls in case she needed me to do something. She would have no problem saying . . . 'I don't understand this at all. This doesn't make sense.' She could be honest when other people were gushing about how beautiful something was when, in reality, it wasn't working. It was a major learning experience, and I learned a ton from the way she would talk honestly to people."

As tempting as it may be to put on your noise-canceling headphones and drown out the people around you, simply listening to how other people work and watching how others respond to them will take you so much further.

You want to think you know it all in your early jobs, as if admitting that you have things to learn would make you a bad hire. But it's exactly the opposite. You have to allow yourself the freedom to experiment, iterate, and explore. Which means that it won't always be high-fives and gold stars on your work, but your ideas will get stronger and your perspective on the business will get broader.

YOU ARE A SPONGE—SOAK IT ALL UP

❶ Don't be a creepy lurker, but take every opportunity to listen in on the ways the more senior folks in your office do their jobs. How do they talk on the phone? What sort of follow-up do they do after meetings? How do they talk to their bosses?

❷ Keep your eyes open for the secret handshakes of your office. Does the boss send handwritten thank-yous? Is she scheduling lunches with folks inside and outside the office? Do meetings start with a little friendly chitchat, or do they get down to business ASAP? Is the junior-staffer lunch collective looked down upon by the senior team or seen as good networking? When you start to understand how business works, you can make it work for you.

❸ Try it all on for size. Sometimes, the weirdest tricks feel awkward at first but turn out to be wildly effective. One Badass Babe used to sit to the right of her boss in every meeting so she'd be her "right-hand man," and she actually got a lot more attention and assignments that way.

BTW, listening shouldn't simply stop after your first gig. At 24 years old, Hannah was hired at a sleepy media company to be the young gun and shake things up. But she quickly learned that acting like she had all the solutions actually got in the way of her earning respect from her team and the bosses. "If I could do everything over, I would go the Hillary Clinton route and do a listening tour," she explains. "They brought me in to be an expert, and I was like, well, I am an expert! Let me show you! And then I realized, oh, actually *you're* the experts." It's a tough lesson to learn the hard way. Hannah had to go back and mend some relationships with coworkers who thought she was bossy and entitled. (Note: Cupcakes "just because," picking up the check at happy hour, or simply a very sincere acknowledgment of their expertise in front of other people whose opinions they value does wonders to smooth ruffled feathers!)

STEP THREE:
VOLUNTEER FOR EVERYTHING

So many companies are assembling millennial task forces, innovation think tanks, and reverse-mentoring programs to give you a chance to be heard. You'd think there would be *tons* of opportunity to move up and around. But the truth is that nobody is thinking about you, unless you're *making* them think about you. Even if your company is scouting for the best and the brightest, you have to raise your hand whenever you can to become a valuable part of your team. After the *American Lawyer,* my next big job was at *React,* a news magazine for teens that went into local newspapers across the country. (Our claim to fame was that we were the first US magazine to put the Spice Girls on the cover!) I got the tip about the gig from a woman I knew in the *React* art department who had done a stint at the *American Lawyer,* and then I leveraged my legal reporting expertise to get a gig writing about legal-ish issues for teens: curfew, drinking, and my favorite story, a teen girl who escaped a cult.

After a few months on the job, my boss called us all into the conference room and announced that he wanted to launch a style section. I raced back to my computer and immediately sent him an email asking if I could head it up. I didn't necessarily know how I was going to do it, but that wasn't going to stop me—I could figure that out later. This moment signaled a significant turn in my career. I had been working on very serious features, and here was a chance for me to add new—fun!—responsibilities and to understand an important piece of our business. Even though I had happily

RAISE YOUR HAND CONSTANTLY

❶ When you hear about a new project or program in the works, let your boss know you're interested ASAP, and tell her why you'd be awesome at it. It's also okay to tell her that it would give you a chance to learn something new—she wants to see you grow.

❷ Even if you don't get the assignment right away, simply signaling that you are hungry for more will eventually mean more will come your way.

❸ Don't flake. If you volunteered, it looks very bad if you back out, drop the ball, or put the project at the bottom of your to-do list. Make it a priority even if you're squeezing it in with all your other responsibilities.

snapped up this opportunity, and was still doing my regular reporting duties, I kept raising my hand. You need someone to help shape the content strategy of a new website? I'm your girl. You want someone to go on ad sales calls and represent the editorial department? Me! The more you volunteer, the more likely the higher-ups are to think of you as their can-do girl and the ops will come to you first.

The same held true when I was the boss. I didn't always have a plan for how I was going to dole out responsibility. I wasn't thinking, okay, I'll give project A to Jessica and project B to Morgan. I just knew what I needed done, and it's so much better to give a project to someone who wants it rather than someone who is going to feel that it's yet another annoying assignment. So, if someone pitched herself for a project before I had to spend any energy thinking about whom to assign it to, I'd think, "Great—that's one less thing on my plate. Done!" You can't take the approach, "Oh, my boss knows where to find me if she needs something." There's no waiting to be tapped if you want to get ahead.

STEP FOUR:
WORK FOR A START-UP

You got a job, you volunteered to take on new projects, and you're moving ahead. But if you want to speed up your career path, working at a start-up is the all-access fast pass.

You probably haven't been to brunch in months without sitting at the table with two or three people who are working at start-ups or developing their own entrepreneurial idea. They go on and on about the micro-dramas in their coworking spaces, and they're all consumed by every single detail of their business—they're so deeply connected to the venture, it's almost cultlike. And as annoying as it is to try to understand the intricacies of their life-changing idea when you just want to enjoy your eggs Benedict and bottomless mimosas, it also sounds sort of enticing to be that invested in something. And though it seems *everyone* wants to be at a start-up now, it was also that way in 1999 when I joined the launch team of *CosmoGIRL!** Admittedly, we were a start-up at Hearst, a giant corporation, but the energy of creating something totally new was just as intoxicating. We were basically five young women huddled around an overheated copier who wanted to talk to teenagers in a new way. For me, the best part in those early days was having a hand in *everything:* fashion, beauty, fitness, relationships, leadership. I developed the website and had meetings with corporate. I courted great writers and created new columns. It was so intense that I ate breakfast, lunch, and usually dinner at the office. I slept under a conference

THE START-UP GIG: THE PROS

❶ If you want to fast-track your move from the entry-level waiting room, working for a start-up can give you more responsibility, a bigger title, and a broader experience.

❷ Clear your calendar. Working at a start-up is *all*-consuming. That cultlike feeling is real—you will have to eat, sleep, and breathe the philosophy of your new venture.

❸ A start-up doesn't have to be forever. Get in, learn everything, move on. Ninety percent of start-ups fail, but there's such a culture around celebrating failure these days that you almost feel bad if you don't come out of it with the framework of a good TED Talk.

MAKE FRIENDS IN THE BUSINESS

When I was a young reporter, a bunch of journalists would get together for something called the Press Club. A woman named Laurel Touby, who was always wearing a pink boa, created this community for freelancers, writers, editors, and reporters to hang out and have cocktails. It was a comfortable and fun way to meet other cool people in the business. It turns out that Laurel and I lived near each other, and we became friendly—running into each other at the gym or the coffee shop. Over iced lattes one day, I suggested that her networking group should go online. I was running an indie website as a side hustle (see Chapter 4), so I offered to help her make that happen. The little Press Club meetings went online, became Mediabistro, and eventually sold to a big company for a fortune. I was thrilled to have been there at the beginning of her career and to have played some small part in launching her massive business. Laurel repaid the favor by thinking of me when she first heard that Hearst Magazines wanted to launch a new teen magazine—*CosmoGIRL!*—and making the right introduction.

That's how networking actually works. I didn't get recommended for the job because of a quick connection I made over watered-down drinks at some industry event. This transaction happened because we had developed a real relationship, we trusted each other, and we each understood what the other chick had to offer. I saw an opportunity I could help her with, and I did. Later on, when something juicy came up, she passed it along to me. Forget about walking into a room full of people trying to balance a glass of wine in one hand and business cards in the other. Just make friends with people you genuinely like in the business, and let the connections happen from there.

table more than once so that I could edit copy in the middle of the night when it came back from production. My life was a mess, but I embraced it because what we were doing felt *meaningful*. At any other magazine where the paths were more well-worn, I would have had to pick a lane and stay in it. Creating a magazine from scratch was like going from zero to 60 in 3.5—fast, fast, fast.

When you're in the early stages of building your career, that's what working at a start-up can do for you, too. When the resources are lean and the ideas are huge, you get a chance to try everything, to see how much you can handle, to learn that you can deal with a tremendous amount of stress and pressure and still

TIPS FROM CHICKS
AT THE TABLE

HOW MEAGHAN O'CONNOR CONVINCED ME TO HIRE HER

"When I was interviewing to be Ann's assistant at *Seventeen*, my dad said, 'There are a million girls who want this job. So why you?' That stuck with me, and I decided I was going to prove that I was the one in a million by doing something out of the ordinary. I put together a presentation called 'Five Reasons I Should Be Your Assistant.' I put in all the talking points from the interview to show I was really paying attention. It was a huge risk, and I was walking a thin line, but I was close enough that it turned out to be a success. I got hired."

thrive. Plus, you're probably going to have a much bigger title than you would at a traditional company, which will help you level up for your next gig. Score! Working at a start-up is like training for an Ironman. And when you cross the finish line, you're stronger, leaner, clearer, and ready to move on to bigger and better things.

STEP FIVE:
WORK FOR A LEGENDARY BRAND

I know it's sexy and fun to move around from job to job, but I stayed at *CosmoGIRL!* for almost 8 years. I was up for other roles, but I never found one that felt like it would be as meaningful—to the audience or to me personally. But then along came *Seventeen*.

After working at a start-up with that underdog mentality, I stepped into a job at a legendary brand feeling like I'd traded in a rickety IKEA kitchen stool for an iconic Eames executive chair. Emails were responded to faster, meetings got moved around less, big ideas were easier to execute because no one needed to be convinced about the power of the brand or the importance it held in young women's lives. Inevitably, when I met someone new, she would tell me how transformative *Seventeen* had been in her life, or her mother's or her grandmothers. Even Oprah said it had been her favorite magazine! And I felt a tremendous responsibility to create a magazine that was just as relevant and important to this generation of young women—your generation.

There's a tremendous power in working for a big brand-name company that's different from the sizzle of working for a scrappy start-up. Working at a big brand puts you in a position to see how high your ideas can fly. It's extraordinary to watch ideas soar when a lot of muscle is put behind them, and it's a validating experience that everyone should have.

THE HARD WORK IS HAPPENING

Every day at your job brings new excitement and new possibilities—but it also feels like there is constantly something new to master.

Pay attention to the way people respond to you. It's a giant feedback loop: Your ideas are good, but could your presentations be sharper? You're great with clients, but don't get too chummy—it's business! You handled that crisis well, but don't forget to keep the higher-ups filled in. It's hard to imagine a time when you'll feel totally in control and doing your job feels like second nature. There's always another step to follow, another skill to tackle, and on it goes. We do the hard work in private, in preparation for stepping onto the big stage.

Right now, you're doing all the hard work. You agonize over proposals. Was it the best it could be? Did you miss something? And you're wondering if your new outfit signals that you're the chick to watch. Or can everyone tell that your expensive new shoes are paired with a dress from Target?

But something happens when you're intensely focused on the details of your work. The bigger pieces slowly but surely come into place, and suddenly, you're prepared to step onto the big stage. You might still be as nervous as hell before your presentation, but this time, everyone is just seeing the badass idea you've presented. And after that presentation, you feel bigger and ready for more. Each new skill you master means you're ticking off a box. You ran that meeting like a boss? Done. What's next? There's no going back to the beginning. You'll never have to get that first job again, and every move you make from that moment on—whether it's taking a job at an interesting start-up, building a big side project from scratch, or working at a legendary brand you've always admired—you're making headway. With each new skill you master, each time you show you can kick ass, you're one click closer to feeling like that superconfident chick who knows how to do it all. And the best part? You'll feel that way all the time.

HOW DO I ASK FOR A RAISE?

Alexandra Dickinson is so passionate about making sure that you're getting paid what you're worth that she founded her own biz, Ask for It, where she empowers clients to ask for what they deserve!

Know Your Goals

Take yourself out of the job you're in and imagine where you want to be in 5 years. You don't need to know exactly how you'll get there, you just need to know where you want to be. Now, what skills will you need to step into that gig? Do you need to manage people, have responsibility for a budget, add some new skills to your CV, or even shadow someone in another division for a broader perspective on your industry? Often, negotiating is about more than strictly salary. All those opportunities have real value that's worth negotiating for.

Know What Your Boss Needs

It's easy to think of asking for a raise as quid pro quo—you've done the work your boss asked you to; you want to get paid for it. But what else does your boss need that's not in the strict letter of your job? Does she need to look good to her boss? Does she need to get more done with fewer resources? When you know what motivates her to make the decisions she has to make in her role, you can have a more impactful conversation about your own job.

Know What Other People Get Paid

No matter how transparent you want to be about your salary, it feels weird to ask your work friends what they make. You don't want to have this conversation over a tipsy happy hour or surprise someone with a blunt ask in the parking lot! Try something like this in a casual convo (ease into it with colleagues who've moved into new jobs): "Hey, congrats on your new gig! I'm up for a review, and I'm asking for a salary increase this year. Would you be willing to share your ballpark salary with me?"

Know Your Worth

Make your case to your boss with hard facts: how much you've made the company, how much you've saved it, what projects you succeeded on, where you helped innovate. Save the money ask until the end of the conversation; by then, your boss will see how valuable you are, and it will seem only fair to give you a proper raise!

4

WHAT'S YOUR SIDE HUSTLE?

**HOW A SECOND (OR THIRD!)
GIG CAN MAKE YOU STRONGER,
SMARTER, AND MORE IN
CONTROL OF YOUR DESTINY**

very Badass Babe has faced that moment when the gloss of your first job starts to wear thin and you feel the Itch. You're not unhappy, exactly. Just a little dissatisfied, with a smidge of anxiety brewing below the surface. There's this nagging question that keeps pulling your focus: Is this all there is? The Itch is similar to the one you get when you're dating someone who is *nice*—the sex is fine, he knows the good restaurants, and tells clever stories at parties. But you find yourself wishing he were taller, sweeter, more assertive, kinder to waitresses, less into where his coffee beans are grown, or more into traveling. You suddenly realize the relationship doesn't quite mesh with the vision you have of yourself. There must be something bigger out there for you. That's the Itch.

Sound familiar?

I have no doubt that you hustled your ass off to line up for your first big job. If anyone was looking for the ultimate summer intern, there you were, memorizing everyone's coffee orders on week one, taking notes in every meeting, and asking your supervisor for mini-reviews every 4 weeks. You know your leadership skills are amazing, so you showed them off by organizing a food drive for a local homeless shelter. Downtime? You tore through *Lean In* and *#GirlBoss*, and you studied the Everygirl's career profiles and Levo League's "Finding Your Passion" and "Building an All-Star Network." You networked like crazy, and your interview outfit, while appropriate, had the right dash of personal flare. The entire process might have taken longer than you'd expected, but it happened. You got a Job. Hello, biweekly salary!

On day one, you had just about everything to learn, and you gave it your all. You mastered the basics, including some of the weird office politics, like who was allowed to be seen having lunch with whom. Your boss's boss knows your name now, and you feel a tiny spark every time she says it in a meeting. And while you still work through lunch more often than not, you've slowly graduated from the sad daily desk salad to an occasional lunch out. That workplace where you were once the new kid is much less of a mystery. You're more in control and have earned some domain. But instead of giving yourself a pat on the back for successfully navigating the tricky waters of the entry-level job, you're wondering . . . what else is there? Where is that next big thing? And how do I make it happen *right now*? You know you have more to offer than the taskiness of your job demands, so why doesn't everyone else?

You've definitely got the Itch.

SYMPTOMS OF THE ITCH: SIGNS YOU NEED A SIDE HUSTLE

❶ Your after-work cocktail banter with friends is morphing from chats about new projects to a bitch fest about that annoying chick who is so obviously sucking up to your boss and blocking your spotlight.

❷ Your boozy weekend brunches with girlfriends are being phased out in your new quest to be Productive, Productive, Productive.

❸ You bought a mug that says, "Good things come to those who hustle!"

❹ You've reached a point where your role as head of operations (BTW, you know that despite the fancy title, you're technically the office manager, receptionist, and head of human resources all in one) doesn't feel worth bragging about anymore.

❺ You've sent late night LinkedIn requests to Lena Dunham, Gabrielle Bernstein, and Oprah!

The Itch

That moment when the gloss of your first job
wears thin and you're a little dissatisfied, with a
smidge of anxiety brewing just below the surface.
It's like that feeling you get when you're dating
someone who is *nice*—the sex is fine, he knows
restaurants, and tells clever stories at parties.
But you find yourself wishing he was taller,
sweeter, more assertive, kinder to waitresses,
or less into where his coffee beans are grown.

You already know that my unglamorous first job as an assistant at the *American Lawyer* magazine turned out to be an amazing learning experience. I was doing your standard entry-level stuff in the beginning: dutifully answering the phones, filing reports, and ordering lunch for my boss (a scoop of tuna salad on iceberg lettuce at 11:30 a.m. Every. Single. Day.). Even though I knew I still had a ton to learn, and I was in the right place to learn a lot of it, I was desperate to have my own domain.

ENTER THE SIDE HUSTLE

Did I know exactly what I wanted to do with my career? Not really, but I knew it was more than re-reporting other writers' stories. So my boyfriend, best guy friend, and I teamed up to create a "downtown" website with an edgy point of view on being young and making your way in the world. We crafted our own lineup, did our own photo shoots, recruited young writers, and paid them in regular pizza and chili nights at my place. (My chili recipe was classic broke-girl ingenuity: a can of black beans, a can of red beans, a can of white beans, and a jar of salsa! Don't knock it till you've tried it!) Suddenly, I had leapfrogged from an assistant to the editor-in-chief of my own publication. I was still answering to my *American Lawyer* editors during the day, but by night, writers were answering to me. And more importantly, I established myself in this digital world that my bosses were still struggling to figure out.

THE SIDE HUSTLE IS ALL ABOUT YOU

The side hustle is like the fast track to a job where you are center stage. Okay, so you're still in a supporting role at your day job, but at your side hustle, you are Beyoncé. You have your very own team of assistants—your backup dancers—following your every move. There is a wind machine blowing your hair just so, and every word that comes out of your mouth is brilliant. Sounds good, right? Remember when everyone thought Destiny's Child was the greatest thing ever?

IT'S NOT ABOUT THE MONEY

Before I show you exactly how a side hustle can make you stronger, smarter, hotter, better in bed, and more in control of your destiny, you need to be completely clear on what a side hustle is NOT. A side hustle is not about selling tunic-length sweaters at American Eagle to fund an adventure vacation to Machu Picchu. It is not about bartending on weekends to make extra money to put toward your student loan (listen, I get that you have to pay your bills and your desire to do that is definitely admirable, but please refer back to the section in Chapter 3 on how to ask for a raise before spending your precious Saturday nights pouring fireball shots for brogrammers). Nor is it the babysitting gig you take to suck up to your boss. A side hustle is not about making extra money.

A side hustle is also not anything that falls under the umbrella of your current day job. But wait—you finally convinced your boss to let you be in charge of your company's new Snapchat marketing campaign, and it's taking up a ton of your time but it's going to be amazing and just the thing to get you noticed? Awesome. Well done. I'm sure you'll nail it. But taking on extra responsibilities at work is not a side hustle—that's smart negotiating in your career.

67

Hello, "Bootylicious"? Could it get any better than that? Apparently Beyoncé thought so, and she had a much bigger vision for herself. And look what happened when she bet on a solo career. Your side hustle is your opportunity to ditch the girl band and prepare to be the Star.

IT DOESN'T HAVE TO BE THE NEXT BIG THING

Obviously, there are no guarantees. Could your star turn be less than magical? Yes—just ask Nicole Scherzinger. Nicole was part of the sexy all-girl group Pussycat Dolls, who had everyone singing "Don't Cha" circa 2005. She tried her hand at a solo career and found herself sitting at the judges table during the 10th season of *The X Factor UK*. Not bad, but not Beyoncé.

So yeah, your side hustle might not be the Next Big Thing, but so what? Your side hustle isn't about actually conquering the world, it's about honoring the fact that you want to do something bigger and giving yourself a shot. Your side hustle isn't about the steady, well-paying job your parents envision for you, and it isn't about some wild moonshot dream your boyfriend thinks you should do together. It's all about you and scratching the Itch. It's your turn to be in control.

My indie website evaporated eventually, but it didn't matter. The feeling of running my own show made me even more ambitious in my career. My website showed me that I was capable in ways that my day gig hadn't tapped into (yet), and my confidence bloomed at work. When my *job*-job started to become as engaging and rewarding as my side hustle, I knew it was time to close up shop at the website and refocus on moving ahead at work.

Let's be honest: Your boss probably isn't that interested in the ways you're reinventing vegan baking or the next frontier of beauty influencers. She has her own strategic agenda, and she needs you to execute her vision. And that's important too. You want to be in a place where you're learning how the business world works, how big ideas rise to the top within a corporate structure, and how to be heard and move ahead. There's tremendous value in working your way up in a company . . . and frankly, there's tremendous virtue in collecting a regular check and paying your bills. Nothing will drain your confidence faster than being in debt and not knowing how you'll get out of it.

Keep the day job, but recognize that we've moved beyond the idea that one gig can be your everything. Maybe your side hustle is an expression of your passion, or maybe it's a way for you to learn some new skills on your own time. Maybe your side hustle is a huge long-shot, but the risk is worth the promise of a massive Facebook IPO–like reward on the other end. The bottom line is, when your regular job makes you feel small and inadequate in the way that only a highly structured, hierarchical, top-down job can, your side hustle can make you feel like a badass. And even if you're feeling stretched thin by your day job, you owe it to yourself to carve out at least a little time for something that makes you feel confident, capable, excited, engaged, and *in charge*.

WHEN YOUR SIDE HUSTLE IS YOUR CALLING CARD

I meet a lot of young women at media industry events, networking happy hours, keynotes I give for women's groups, and fireside chats at universities. These are young women who've paid for their tickets and gotten up early on a Saturday or stayed at work late on a Thursday to glean a few more secrets or soak up a little more inspiration about their careers. For the most part, these young women are polished and poised. They get regular blowouts and manicures. They have researched me and my work and come prepared with well-thought-out questions. They are earnest and serious . . . but Savannah is not like any of them. I meet her when she breezes into my house for a Badass Babes dinner in a silky shorts romper—emphasis on *short*—with her slightly wild hair and softly smudged eyeliner. I see a glimpse of a gold body chain slipping into her cleavage (cleavage!). While other Badass Babes request French electronica or the National over cock-tails before dinner, Savannah queues up '90s Summer Jams on Pandora. "I want to hear some LFO throwback tunes," she exclaims as she refills her wineglass. Savannah exudes the kind of cool-girl sexy confidence that makes men melt into goopy puddles and makes women want to grill her for all her secrets.

But don't let her easy-breezy persona fool you; Savannah is *ambitious*. It's not the ambition that comes with a big degree from a fancy university and a LinkedIn page of well-placed connections. She went to a state school and changed majors every other semester. First, chemical engineering, then journalism, then event production and business. And life after college has been more of the same sort of random walk—a pupu platter of jobs to fill her days and pay the bills: a restaurant gig, a mindless entry-level marketing job, a stint as a Big Sister on the weekends, and Pilates instructor train-ing. She longs for the real deal: a solidly paying job that also gets her excited about work every morning. But for now, she's taking the pieces she can get and making do the best way she can. BTW: There's a boyfriend . . . for now. "He works 8:30 a.m. to 6:00 p.m., so I will go days and days without seeing him," she says. "We're probs going to break up over it, realistically speaking."

Everything changed, she explains, when she met Eric. "Eric was launching this cool website for 20-somethings, and he wanted to get me involved as an editor." Ah! Finally, she thought, this was her chance to catapult herself out of the mind-wasting grind of serving beers to entry-level finance dudes and ditch the soul-sucking marketing gig. She was not going to let this opportunity slip by. "I started spewing ideas at him nonstop until he knew I was serious, and he finally asked me to be the editor-in-chief," she says. Sounds like important work, right? She's assigning stories, managing writers, and editing copy. But here's the thing: It's a brand-new venture with no capital whatsoever, so Savannah is doing this big job for *free*.

The allure of this side hustle is that it gives Savannah something to brag about over cocktails. She sparkles when she talks about her first big career high. One of her writers was assigned a piece on a buzzy new documentary, and in the middle of the movie trailer, right after quotes from major media outlets like *Rolling Stone* and the *New York Times,* was a quote from *her* website. She knew right then that she was starting to make her mark. "When I saw that, I really lost it!"

And before you dismiss this site as simply some vanity project, note that it gives her credibility in a field that isn't so easy to break into. "I didn't get a degree in journalism, so I can't put it on my résumé to impress HR at the big companies," she explains. "But now I oversee 65 people." They work for free, just like she does—it seems like everyone is hustling to make a name for themselves. Savannah's goal is to ultimately get paid as an editor—at her current website, if it ever starts making money, which she knows is a long shot, or at a more established outlet. But she's worried that she's skipping steps and not actually prepared for one of the more traditional jobs. Usually, I tell young women that I couldn't care less where they went to school or what they studied. When I hire someone, I'm looking for ways that they stand out from the crowd and how they pursued leadership opportunities, even if it was only their sorority's spring fundraiser. I'm looking for the passion that Savannah has in spades.

But Savannah is still at that early stage when she's filling out applications for jobs rather than sending off her CV and a carefully crafted cover letter to the editor. It's the lack of degrees and actual job experience that keeps her from getting past the HR gatekeeper. And so Savannah's side hustle is the thing she's banking on to give her something meaningful to say in those cover letters. It's the thing she leads with at cocktail parties and networking events. She has serious-looking business cards with her name right above "Editor-in-Chief." It's the first entry on her LinkedIn. Marketing and bartending are paying her bills; the side hustle is paying in experience and self-respect. For Savannah, the side hustle has opened a door that she's been knocking on for years. She's been on the outside, looking through the window at a clique of superpolished media women who've make their career paths look so effortless. They seem to know all the right people, get all the calls for new positions, say the right things in all their emails without rewriting them a thousand times. Though she's in the room with them now, she still feels like an outsider. But many of those superpolished women who are a little further ahead of Savannah have been plotting this career path since they were in freshman journalism lecture halls, and they wish they could be as certain about their *passion* as Savannah is about hers.

WHEN YOUR SIDE HUSTLE BECOMES YOUR CAREER

Tammy Tibbetts is one of those girls who looks like she's had her career path perfectly mapped out. She's serious to the point of being studious at work. She has a soft voice and uses exactly as many words as she needs to make her point. You won't catch her nervously gabbing away or just filling air during a meeting. Her big, soft eyes don't dart around the room to see who else is coming in—she's focused. Plus, her hair is awesomely shiny and always in place. Tammy started as an intern at *Seventeen,* and her job was basically to clean the beauty closet. But she was tenacious and persistent, gathering experience and moving up until she hit the sweet spot: becoming the social media director of *Seventeen.* Social media was starting to explode, and everyone wanted to know what Tammy instinctually understood: the new ways to connect with young people about the things they care about. Her gig at *Seventeen* was one that a million girls would have killed for. But Tammy had been incubating a side project that spoke deeply to her. Little did she know that her commitment to girls and education would take her from a job at *Seventeen* to launching her own nonprofit.

Tammy was the first person in her family to graduate college, and she was acutely aware of how much opportunity her education had afforded her. She also knew that there were more than 50 million girls living in the developing world who wouldn't get the kind of education she had. Tammy was incredibly excited about an idea she had for a social media campaign that would get other millennial women involved in fundraising to help girls in developing countries receive scholarships for primary and secondary school. So when Tammy's side project started ramping up, and funding was coming in, she came to see me about dialing back her hours. My response was, "Um, no." At this point, I was in boss mode. Her side hustle was not part of my strategic plan. Social media was a high priority, and I needed a director who was available full-time. Her response was a respectful but clear, "No, what I'm doing is bigger, and that's where I'm going to spend my time. So, I'm leaving." I admit I didn't understand it then, but now I see that Tammy knew she could go out there

---

TIPS FROM CHICKS AT THE TABLE

HOW TAMMY KNEW IT WAS TIME TO BREAK UP WITH HER DAY JOB

"When you get to the point where you can no longer do your real job and your side hustle at 100 percent, you have to be honest with yourself. I remember starting to make mistakes in my day job at *Seventeen*, and that's when I knew I had to make a choice. *Seventeen* deserved someone who did 100 percent in my role, and She's the First needed someone with 100 percent focus if it was going to take off. You have to stay ahead of the curve, and you don't want to get fired. Your reputation is of utmost importance, and you want to take those relationships along with you.

When I left *Seventeen*, I had just gotten the first major gift and corporate sponsorship for She's the First, and that was another reason I knew it was time. Once others are investing in your plans, you need to make the biggest investment and have the confidence to take the leap.

I also believe that if you help find and train your replacement, and try to leave the company in a better place than when you started, it should all work out!"

and make the world work like she wanted it to work. "I guess I thought I had no choice but to do it, and I needed to do it because there are girls and young women around the world who have no choices, and what did I have to lose?" Tammy reasons. "If it failed, and I couldn't raise the operating funds for us to grow and have a staff, I probably could have gotten hired again in the magazine business. So, I gave myself that year to see what would happen."

Tammy named her program She's the First and launched it with a YouTube video, hoping to engage millennials and students to end global poverty, one small contribution at a time. Now, she's on *Fortune's* "30 under 30" list and has provided scholarships to 800 young women in eleven countries. "When I launched our YouTube video, I didn't think it was going to be my career path," she says. "It was how it snowballed that kind of pulled me in that direction. I always thought it would be a campaign that I do on the side of my dream, which was working at a magazine. It just happened to me."

She's the First has provided more than 2,200 scholarships for girls who may not have had the opportunity to go to school at all without Tammy's idea. However, Tammy is quick to say that you don't have to start a nonprofit to make a huge impact. "I don't want people to look at my story, which is so unconventional, and think they have to work at a nonprofit to make a difference. They can work within corporations, start their own businesses that are profitable, and donate back and make a bigger difference in the world than if they try to start something from scratch."

It's hard not to be inspired by Tammy—after all, she's literally changing girls' lives. But she took the path ahead of her one step at a time. And with every new contact she made, every new college chapter she recruited, every new benefactor who supported the initiative, her vision for what she could achieve got bigger. The quiet girl with the big eyes who used to sweep the beauty-closet floor found a deep well of confidence that has helped her move her part-time side hustle onto the national stage and have a global impact. And if you need further proof of the power of Tammy's vision and her gentle but firm approach to business, I am now a proud advisor to She's the First.

WHEN YOUR PERFECT JOB IS KILLING YOU

Genevieve's day starts off with pantyhose. Every single day, she rifles through her drawer until she finds a pair that doesn't have snags. She carefully slides them on before putting on a dark suit and a practical pair of closed-toed shoes. The dress code at the fancy Wall Street bank where she ended up right after graduation is no joke. When Genevieve was getting her dual degree, she was focused on the payoff—that Big Job in finance with the matching paycheck that would make her parents proud. It didn't occur to her that she might want something more.

She's only in her early 20s but quick to describe her position as "pretty high-powered" and admits to hauling in a hefty salary. So what's the problem? "I found that it's not that fulfilling a career. You are just sort of moving stuff around on PowerPoint and analyzing numbers that don't really impact anything," she says. So while Genevieve is earning the big bucks (albeit while adhering to the world's biggest drag of a dress code), she can't help envying friends who work in a looser, more energetic start-up culture. "In cubicles, you feel trapped. And for a 20-something who knows there is so much energy and excitement in other industries, everyone in my office is like, 'What am I doing here? Why am I here?' Everyone looks miserable, and people are dropping like flies."

As much as she'd like to quit, Genevieve admits that her parents and boyfriend, who all went down traditional career paths, are piling on major pressure for her to stay put. "Even my dad was like, 'You can only leave the bank when you get married.' If I didn't have these voices in every direction telling me to make sure I don't get fired, I probably would have quit already."

While Genevieve's journey to her career was a straight shot from point A to point B, she craves the twists and turns that mark her friends' résumés. "Finance is just the path of least resistance when you go to a school like the one I went to; everyone does it," she says with a resigned sigh. Genevieve admits that the career counselor at her school pointed her toward finance. "But what no one ever talked about is what happens when you get there," she says. "You get that perfect job you've been told will give you power, money, and security, and you *hate* it." Genevieve wasn't quite ready to leave that "perfect job," so she started a side hustle that helped lift her spirits and put her finance background skills to good use.

YOUR OWN PRIVATE REBELLION

Genevieve's journey from school straight to a bland cubicle inspired her to launch a networking-event series to help others who've landed in the same boat—those who worked hard for a cushy finance gig, only to face major disappointment. With the guidance of a legendary New York connector who saw the potential to tap into a younger generation, Genevieve created a casual, comfortable environment where people could gather for coffee, treats, and talks by interesting entrepreneurs or experts. The overall idea was to show that there are other paths beyond business school and finance.

Once a month, Genevieve sheds her blazer for a pencil skirt and a body-hugging black cashmere sweater—classic chic, and no pantyhose! She hosts the events with dynamic speakers and organic food from a local caterer. (The catering company is a friend's side hustle!) "The people who come to speak at my networking events are the people I admire. The people who have had the guts to follow their dreams and passions full-time and make something out of it," Genevieve explains as her eyes light up. "I just don't see the same role models in the corporate world." She didn't have the mentors she needed at work, so she created a massive network of her own.

Genevieve figured that she couldn't be the only person who followed her life plan perfectly but then faced disappointment. "It's hard to figure out what to do outside of consulting and finance," she explains. "A lot of people want to do *something* impactful. But there's no resource that tells you how to do that, to show you what a career looks like outside of an easy corporate path." Genevieve might not see things the way her dad and boyfriend do, but their message about playing it safe is something she hasn't exactly been able to ignore. Her side hustle is like her own private rebellion—it's a way for her to dance on the fringes of all these expectations, build something that she's truly excited about, and surround herself with people who inspire her.

Genevieve's networking events are not some loosey-goosey drink-and-bitch fests. There's a business plan, strategic advisors, and seed investors. The crowd is made up of young men and women who are looking for advice on how to shape their own side hustles and start-ups. Genevieve said she would quit her stodgy office job in a heartbeat to focus on her networking events full-time if she could. But even if it's her mini-rebellion, she's not the kind of chick who likes a high-wire act with no safety net. "I don't want to be at my banking job. But I need to be there because it pays my bills," she says. "I've been told by people to quit. But it doesn't make sense to me. I'd just be more scared and desperate."

No matter how much you want to break free from your corporate job, you have to respect Genevieve's desire to carve her own path on her own terms. And, for her, that means taking carefully calculated steps to leave her steady gig. "I want to leave when my events are making me *twice* what I'm making in my finance job," she says boldly. If making a big move will be full of stress and fear, then make sure you can see the ground beneath your feet before you jump. In Genevieve's case, it's almost like she's seriously dating her side hustle. She knows they click, but she wants to see whether she and her side hustle are truly compatible before she fully commits.

SOMETIMES, A SIDE HUSTLE IS JUST A SIDE HUSTLE

When you pinpoint your passion, you *think* you want to be all in right away. But imagine your passion is yoga—you were hooked from your very first sun salutation. You splurge on a monthly pass to the yoga studio, and nearly every morning begins with a vinyasa sequence. Soon enough, you are obsessed with crazy-angle poses and handstands. Nothing makes you happier than smoothly sailing through a series of poses in an airy, light-filled loft—you could do it for hours. You start to find that you're never without your yoga mat, and all you want to talk about over coffee with friends (actually, hot water with lemon, for you) is how life-changing yoga has been. Then your lightbulb moment: "You should sell all your belongings and move to an ashram," you think. That's how passionate you are about yoga!

Wait—what?!

Before you book your plane tickets to India, there are about a million middle points to explore—become a yoga instructor, write a blog about yoga, create a line of organic yoga mats, lobby Congress for yoga to be a part of middle school physical education . . . you get the idea. Just because you are passionate about something doesn't mean that you have to make it your whole life. If there's no clear vision for your side hustle to be your main gig, that's okay. Your side hustle is about scratching that pesky Itch. It's quieting that voice in the back of your head that's wondering when it's your turn for bigger and better things. Once that noise is turned off, your focus can turn to how to get there.

WHAT'S NEXT FOR YOU?

As much as I see your Itch and want to help you deal, not that long ago, I was the boss lady who probably wasn't overly concerned about your Itchiness. Did I want you to succeed? Hell yes. I wanted you to nail that dream and then find a bigger one and do the same. I think most bosses mean it when they say that they want their employees to be happy. I know I did. But I had a major magazine to run: I had editors and writers to manage, advertisers to keep happy, photo shoots and countless meetings to attend. That didn't leave much time for me to have in-depth chats about how to make you feel like you're "contributing more" to the magazine. You want someone to give you a plan to follow that leads you right to the attention you deserve. But the truth is that you have to make your own plan; it's not your boss's job—or anyone else's—to figure it all out for you.

I recently had coffee with Lindsey, who is beyond irritated with her job situation. After a fairly brutal initiation at a hot new start-up, she doesn't feel like a total disaster anymore. In fact, she's started to feel like her opinion is being valued and plum assignments are coming her way. She's super-proud of her last project and knows that big things are right around the corner. Finally.

WHAT KIND OF SIDE HUSTLE IS RIGHT FOR YOU?

❶ THE SOLUTION HUSTLE Is there a problem you wish someone would solve for you? Other people surely feel the same way. Solve it yourself and make a side hustle out of helping others who have the same problem.

❷ THE SAVE-THE-WORLD HUSTLE Is there a big global issue that keeps you up at night? Turn tackling that social issue into a side hustle—support a cause or volunteer at an organization that's already working on it.

❸ THE SISTERHOOD HUSTLE Do you have a friend who has an excellent business idea but doesn't know how to execute it? Collaborate with her and help make her idea a reality.

❹ THE SECRET HUSTLE What's your special talent? Do you have a perfectly fine day job, but at night you're throwing fab dinner parties with delicious food and buzzy conversation? Or, maybe all your friends are asking you to design their WordPress sites because you're a superpro. Your secret talent can be transformed into a side hustle.

❺ THE CEO HUSTLE Do you love your job but wish you were the boss? Create a side hustle where you're in charge!

The
New Chick

A recent hire who doesn't have a drop of shyness about voicing her opinion in meetings, booking one-on-one lunches with the senior staffers during her first week, or claiming the prime summer Fridays. She is treading on your territory and acting like she owns the place.

And then, enter the New Chick.

Lindsey could not get over the recent hire who didn't have a drop of shyness about voicing her opinion in meetings, booked one-on-one lunches with the senior staffers during her first week, and claimed the prime summer Fridays. "She's been there 2 weeks, and she's acting like she owns the place!" she sobbed to me. This might seem like jealousy or garden-variety bitchiness, but I see it as a signal that you're too cautiously guarding old territory and that you need to show your bosses that you're ready to break new ground. Waste no energy over people who may or may not "own the place." That chick is still working on the 1.0 version of what a good worker looks like, while you have turned the corner and are about to unveil version 2.0. She's marching into your territory, but you've already conquered it. You're ready to move on, and she's only making your Itch worse. But, rather than let your dissatisfaction turn you against her, devote your energy to places where it can make a difference—new projects, new clients, new side hustles. So what if the new girl thinks she's as good as you? What else is next *for you*? Don't wait for the next rung; hustle yourself to wherever it is you want to go.

Look, the Itch is the worst. But it's what stokes the fire of your ambition. Your hunger drives you to seek out something bigger and better. But sometimes it's so overwhelming to know that there's more you can do and to not see a way to show the world how amazing you are that you just want to get under the duvet and eat an extra-large bag of barbecue potato chips. In those moments, remind yourself that if it wasn't for that Itch, you'd be just another girl at work sitting quietly, waiting for a promotion. That's not you. You're the chick who brushes off the crumbs and finds a new way to show the world how amazing you really are. And you do it again and again.

5

#SQUADGOALS

MAKE YOUR CREW
WORK FOR YOU

It's lonely being a leprechaun. That's what Grace's boss calls her because she's such a rare breed: a millennial senior executive in a traditional corporate environment and a woman of color. She usually loves all the expectations—and the responsibilities—that come with standing out from the crowd. She's on major philanthropic boards and gets invites to every important industry dinner (and to have exclusive, intimate after-hours drinks with the real power players too). She has a massive list of contacts—there's almost nothing she can't make happen.

And then there are the times when the responsibility that comes with being a leprechaun just plain sucks. One late night at the office in 2014, after a brutal round of corporate downsizing, Grace found herself with a long list of people she had to send official notice that they were being laid off and another long list of reporters she had to call back in the morning with an "everything's fine" message. It's the kind of corporate busywork/dirty work that can drain your will to live. No one's 16-year-old dream for the Big Life revolves around alerting 200-plus people that their COBRA benefits will expire in 90 days and that their 401(k)s are at risk. As the clock struck midnight, alone at the office, she let her head fall heavily into her hands and felt the tremendous weight of the day and the pressure of her job. This was not the braggy "it's lonely at the top" kind of loneliness. This was isolation. "Here I am at the office at midnight, and *everyone* hates me," she remembers thinking. And so she picked up the phone and dialed. Not her boyfriend, not her mother . . . but her friend and colleague Brandi. Brandi had been through it before—she's the kind of seasoned industry vet who gets the best table at the see-and-be-seen restaurants and remembers everyone by name as she makes her way through a room.

She's brassy and bold, but her brashness is softened by a tremendous admiration for young women who are just starting to put their names on the map. Women like Grace. And so, 20 minutes later, Grace found herself on Brandi's roof deck, staring into the glittering lights of New York City with a glass of good cabernet in hand. Together, they strategized on how Grace could get through this hellish moment, move out of the corporate trenches, capitalize on her deep experience, elevate herself, and craft a new vision for her future: They would call Mel, who was going through exactly the same thing at her bigwig job, for some immediate career triage. Then Jordan, for some social-responsibility insight—maybe there was a massive philanthropy that needed Grace's help? And Sydney, for an entrepreneur's POV. It was too late to place those calls, but just reminding herself that the chicks in her squad are there for her and so invested in her success and happiness gave her the energy to get up and face work again in the morning.

"It's not forced," Grace explains. "It's a community, a sisterhood. We want each other to succeed. But first and foremost, we want each other to be *happy*." It's a funny concept for Grace to think about what makes her happy. Grace's mom, who held down two jobs to put Grace through school, couldn't imagine walking away from a six-figure job—and tells Grace so. And Grace's boyfriend, who loves her deeply, lets his business school management training lead when faced with a career crisis. He has made strategy maps and spreadsheets to get clarity for Grace's next move. It's nice to have him on her side, Grace says, but it's not exactly what her soul is craving. "Since college, I've been climbing a big corporate ladder, and very rarely did I pause to ask, 'Is this making me happy?'" Grace says. "My squad cares about my happiness first."

When you think "squad," it's hard not to imagine Taylor Swift—you can't help it. In fact, she practically created the modern idea of the girl gang. Think back to the 2015 VMAs for a sec. Remember that picture of Taylor and her crew? After winning best music video of the year for "Bad Blood," she didn't pose for pictures alone. She was flanked by major Badass Babes Selena Gomez, Gigi Hadid, Hailee Steinfeld, Cara Delevigne, and Karlie Kloss—each one hotter and more awesomely dressed than the next. That picture represents #SquadGoals at its peak. A quick flick through Taylor's Instagram page shows that she's out there having tons of fun with her girls. There's a pic of her and Lena Dunham walking down a NYC street post-brunch, both in quirky outfits; there's one of Taylor with her model friends posing in bikinis on vacay in Maui. And there's a supercute one of her hiking in California with Karlie Kloss, and shopping with Lorde for boots at Free People. So, if Taylor Swift and her squad are all about brunch, vacations, shopping, and baking cookies, they're not so different from your squad, are they? You brunch. You vacay. You bake.

IT'S ABOUT MORE THAN CHAI TEA SUGAR COOKIES

Here's the thing about Taylor's squad: It's tempting to write it all off as some cute pop culture moment, and it might appear to be all about carefully coordinated outfits. But there's actually something much bigger going on than a bunch of A-list girls bonding over homemade chai tea sugar cookies. If you take a closer look, you'll see that each chick in Taylor's squad brings her own unique power to the group. Karlie has created a scholarship to teach coding to girls; Selena is producing a new TV show and investing in a tech start-up; Hailee is nurturing a music career. These Badass Babes are serious about business, and it's *power* that actually connects these women, NOT just the girly fun antics.

So, while you and your squad may not be discussing the various challenges of pulling off an international stadium tour, or producing, writing, and directing the hit HBO show you've created (or maybe you are), it's incredibly important to surround yourself with women who nod their heads yes when you talk about your ambition. Power is not a zero-sum game. If you have power, you don't have to give something up so your friends can be more powerful. When there are more women with power, you create more power—together.

SQUADS PLAY A TOTALLY UNIQUE ROLE IN THE BIG LIFE

It used to be that you'd hash through your work woes with the people you saw every day, à la the characters on *Friends*—a close circle of pals hanging out together all the time. But your network has exploded way beyond the idea of the people you drink coffee with on an overstuffed couch. Today, your tribe is more focused and more powerful, but it still offers sisterhood. When you're doing something hard, like carving a new path for your life, with no clear role models to follow, you need to find people who support you and think your dream is brilliant. Your squad needs to be made up of the chicks who get you *and* your ambition. These are the women who inspire your dreams—and the women you can you turn to when you're barely holding on to a thread of those dreams, and it all feels impossible. You're not trying to slide yourself into some

YOUR FEED OF INSPO

Even if you find yourself on some airless planet surrounded by people who think that you'd be better off sticking with the status quo, you can tap into the Big Life inspo you need on YouTube or Instagram. Purge the noise from your feed—all those party pics of your high-school friends and the ironic musings of some guy you met on a summer immersion trip are draining your energy. Instead, focus on the people who see the world the way you do, who are creating the life you want to emulate. Aspirational can be seriously inspirational.

For example, I follow Jennifer Fisher—an amazing jewelry designer who posts pics of Rihanna sporting her designs and also posts about her endless devotion to her family. Jennifer reminds me how important my family is to my own success. I also swoon a little when YouTuber Meghan Reinks favorites my tweets—she's one of the coolest, prettiest chicks I've ever met, and also happens to be ridiculously funny and goofy. She shows that there's real power in being yourself and in showing that to the world.

Sometimes, all you need is a little inspiration to keep you excited about that Big Life you're building. If looking at Lauren Conrad's gorgeous Pinterest pics of carefully arranged flowers reminds you that your Big Life will have room for such loveliness, great. Or, if Amy Schumer's Instagram page inspires you to honor your dark and silly side, go there. I know what it's like to get lost in the social media rabbit hole while the evening flies by. It's tempting to tell yourself you should be working, exercising, returning emails, cleaning, or doing one of the billion other things that needs to be done instead. But sometimes you need to forget about all the tasks immediately at hand. You need to let yourself laugh hard, marvel at all the amazingness out there, and dream about how your contribution to it all will be funnier, smarter, and even more wonderful.

89

preexisting role, and your squad supports you in that. You've bonded with these babes because you have a common goal: making the world work for you on your terms.

SQUAD BUILDING

I never had a squad until I was much further along in my career. After college, my best friends all scattered. One decided to travel, one relocated to the West Coast for work, and another moved home to save money for law school. The girls at my *American Lawyer* job didn't have much of a vision for their careers—or at least not a vision that connected with me, and frankly, I didn't have much of a vision then either. We would have drinks and talk about our jobs, but not much about what came next. And they were in the same slow-moving boat I was in, so we weren't much help to one another. The other more senior editors who seemed to be moving faster or further than me weren't all that helpful. They were ready for someone to report to them to validate their new authority in the business. I get that, but boy did it suck. No one wants to be hungrily eyeing every move of the person with the cookies, hoping that a little crumb falls their way. I slowly got introduced to a few people outside my immediate work circle. But they were stingy with their cookies too—and occasionally condescending, as if they'd magically figured out what they wanted to do with their lives, how to move ahead, get noticed, and make their dreams come true . . . and how dumb was I not to have also been able to figure it out too! (Weirdly, I reconnected with one of the most condescending of the bunch about 20 years later when I was looking for a different kind of help in my career. Yep! Still condescending. Still acting like her cookies were better than everyone else's. It's just as important to know who is *not* in your squad!)

Listen, it's pretty lonely trying to find your place in the world—and there's no way around that. No matter how many likes you get on your #SundayFunday posts, those probably aren't the people who are going to help you figure out how you're going to make your mark. And you don't want to grind your friendships to the ground with nonstop questions about where you should be going and how you're going to get there. No one wants to be friends with the girl who *only* wants to agonize about how to get ahead in life.

So, how do you find your squad? The moment you meet some badass woman and you find yourself thinking, "Damn, how do I get a little of what she has?" That's someone you want in your squad, so invite her to drinks, or, better yet, tell her you'd love to wingwoman for her at her book club, networking group, favorite spoken-word performance, or other random fun thing that shows you're interested in stuff too!

I've personally always been inspired by the outliers. The girl with killer web skills who wanted to drill water wells in Africa. The copywriter who was working on a novel in her spare time. The freelancer who started a happy hour for other freelancers and then turned it into a multimillion-dollar recruiting business. The philanthropist who acted like a CEO. If I happened to find myself having drinks with these women, I didn't necessarily press them for information. We talked about meetings we'd had, opportunities on the horizon, and new projects in the works. Inevitably, once the business talk was done, we'd turn to dates, Susan Miller horoscopes, or blow-dry secrets. That kind of chitchat wasn't just fluff; it was a way for us to deepen our relationship and to find further common ground. It wasn't traditional networking; we were becoming *friends*. I wasn't looking for mentorship, and I wasn't constantly asking for advice about situations at work—

(continued on page 94)

91

When you're assembling your all-star team, these are the types of Badass Babes you need in your squad!

THE CONNECTOR Instead of saying, "Do you know so-and-so," which can make people feel like a total loser if they have to say no, this chick says, "OMG—you should know so-and-so. I'll introduce you." And you know it's not just empty chitchat, because she opens her phone and puts it on her to-do list right there in front of you. You love this woman for being so generous with her connections, but honestly, knowing you and making the right intros makes her look better too.

THE SUGGESTER Have you ever had lunch with someone and come away with a long to-do list of conferences you have to research, articles you have to read, and products you have to try? That's the Suggester. She'd be exhausting if she wasn't so smart and usually right.

THE SYMPATHY SISTER Everyone needs one chick in her squad who says, "Ugh, that is the worst thing I've ever heard. You poor baby. You deserve better." She simply gives you permission to feel all the feels—which is not celebrated enough, IMHO.

YOUR PLUS ONE She's the ultimate work-event wingwoman. It looks bad if you tote your boyfriend along to all your industry parties and networking cocktails. And your other friends just aren't interested. Your Plus One comes with her own cred, and she knows how to strike up a convo with the power players who intimidate you and when to save you from the cling-ons who won't . . . stop . . . talking.

THE INSIDER This woman is senior, celebrated, well known, and likes you! She'd be your mentor, if she had time for that kind of a formal arrangement. Instead, she's someone you can email (sparingly) if you have a well-thought-out question or need a carefully researched connection request. She probably says you remind her of herself when she was younger—great! Total compliment!

WARNING: STAY AWAY FROM THE DARK CLOUDS

Make it your mission to build a squad of supportive, productive people you admire and respect, and who are all about shedding light—not sucking it out of everyone's day with their constant complaining. When I started at *Seventeen,* there was a small group who gathered by the water cooler to complain. You could practically see the dark cloud around them from down the hall. These people were all about negativity, not about being amazing or coming up with solutions to the stuff that was bugging them. Always remember that no good can come from being a dark cloud or aligning yourself with one. Ditto the social-climbers, who use other women as stepping-stones, and the flakers, who promise stuff but never follow through.

P.S.: THE CHICKS IN YOUR SQUAD ARE NOT YOUR COWORKERS . . . OR YOUR THERAPISTS

To be clear, your relationship with the chicks in your squad is more nuanced than the one you have with your colleagues at work. Sure, you're supportive with the women in your office and you have a regular happy hour, but often you're competing for the same raises and promotions, and so you can't be totally candid with them. Plus, they're focused on the j-o-b . . . not your Big Life hopes and dreams. Your squad shouldn't be mired in your day-to-day, so they can help you see the broader perspective when you're feeling overwhelmed by the tiny details of your crisis du jour. But these chicks aren't your therapists either. You're not spilling every single detail of your life to them. There's closeness and a sisterhood that revolves around your ambition, but the truth is, you're saving your most vulnerable self for your BFFs. You have a different connection with those friends you've known forever. On the other hand, everyone in your squad understands your connection is power and has a vision for the Big Life, not a mutual love of Justin Timberlake or an encyclopedic knowledge of your Tinder-date disasters.

but I knew I could turn to these women if I were facing a sticky situation. Just the fact that they'd veered from what seemed like safe and well-worn paths is what inspired me to take risks in my own life, ask for opportunities, and plant seeds of new ideas. If they could do it, I reasoned, so could I.

For a long time, that was my ad hoc squad. Smart, ambitious women whom I could occasionally tap for a nugget of info or a connection. There was nothing formalized about our meet-ups. That's not how it is now. There's been an explosion of warm, collegial cliques that connect in Facebook groups or meet up in person, like Her Campus chapters, Skimm'bassador groups, and local Levo chapters. They all have the same goal: to help each other succeed.

I'm on the Li.st, a listserv for women in technology and media who trade contacts, offer cheers, and help one another hash through some of the hairiest situations I've ever heard of. One Badass Babe started a group called the Middle Collective for chicks like her who were in the middle of their careers and wanted to help others move up in the world. And Grace turned her own power squad into a proper women's group with multiple chapters in the US and Europe. That's the kind of power player Grace is—it's not enough for her to have a squad; she needs to turn it into a business!

YOUR SQUAD GETS YOU THROUGH THOSE LOSE-THE-FAITH MOMENTS

It would be amazing if your squad simply high-fived you as you leaped from one amazing moment to the next. But even Taylor Swift has a dark night of the soul when she's convinced that she's making the wrong decision, hasn't done enough research, is too far out on a limb . . . I know you've felt that overwhelming anxiety at 4:00 a.m. or the iron fist of stress that settles between your shoulders to remind you how hard it is to do big things. Every Badass Babe has had to deal with self-sabotaging doubt that causes a deep inner ache, and thought about giving up. And while you have a tight-knit crew of girlfriends who didn't think twice about holding your ponytail for you while you puked your guts out in college, it doesn't mean they're necessarily the right people to lean on now. Their dreams aren't always your dreams. You might love them like sisters, but when it comes to conversations about building the Big Life, some weird disconnects or even jealousy can come out in a judgy way. At those moments, you have to realize that sometimes you need to let friends just be your besties—let them do their own thing. And so, when it comes to the complexities of finding your power, don't call your girlfriends . . . call your squad.

NOT EVERYONE HAS TO GET IT

For Amy, it stung a little—okay, *a lot*—when she realized that her friends didn't quite share her vision for the Big Life. But when the hurt emails cleared, she realized that other women were on her side—that's what the chicks in her squad were for.

You wouldn't want to meet Amy in a dark bowling alley—she once took $2,000 off a party promoter at a splashy new bowling spot who thought she couldn't possibly knock down strike after strike after strike (and beer after beer!). That $2,000 funded a girls-only trip to the Bahamas! If people underestimate her, Amy has figured out how to use that to her advantage. She has a quiet smile, her long hair falls in those effortless waves that take most women half the morning to

The Girls
Back Home

That idea that the Girls Back Home are living
in a twilight zone that's void of ambition is a
convenient story we tell ourselves to make our
own struggle feel worth the pain.

create, and at 5 feet 10 inches tall, she's not afraid of sky-high heels. When she was a year out of college, that poise and confidence helped her land a coveted celeb-reporting job that filled her Instagram feed with envy-inspiring pics of Brad Pitt, Reese Witherspoon, and George Clooney. But she's the first to admit that being a red-carpet reporter isn't always as glamorous as it looks. "I'm often standing in a mud puddle for 3 hours in the rain, just waiting for these people to come talk to me for literally 30 seconds."

Amy has always had a clear vision for her Big Life. She went to a top-notch school and graduated a year early so she could move to NYC and start interning. (Take note: In a brilliant move, she convinced her dad to bankroll her first year in the city—cheaper than tuition, she reasoned!) It's not the celebs that excite Amy, but the pride in being the first in her family to move away from their small Southern hometown—to NYC, no less. In high school, she and her best friend raced home from school to binge-watch *Sex and the City* and imagine what it would be like when they were writing for *Vogue* like Carrie or when they ran an art gallery like Charlotte. But now that she's living a version of that dream, she's found that her friends from back home don't always understand her passion and desire for something bigger. "My friends from home are on a very different page than I am. They're all just like, 'Oh, I want to find a boyfriend and get married.' They don't really care what they do for a career," Amy says.

Ahh, recognize that feeling? You have to tread carefully here. That idea that the Girls Back Home are living in a twilight zone that's void of ambition is a convenient story we tell ourselves to make our own struggles feel worth the pain. After all, when you're working 60 hours a week, eating hummus out of the container for dinner, and dating dudes who put you in their phones by hair color, it helps make it a little more okay if you feel like your struggle is more noble than someone else's. You want to say that they took the easy way out by forgoing some overpriced closet-size apartment or by working in their parents' business rather than trying to rise through the ranks at a massive corporation. But the truth is, those girls are plenty ambitious; their vision for the Big Life just doesn't look like yours. And if you're being honest with yourself, that's the part that drives you nuts. We want our friends' lives to be like our lives so that it validates the choices we make. We want someone in the struggle with us. And it feels like a betrayal when it doesn't work out that way.

For Amy, the betrayal came from her best friend. "The summer before college graduation, we interned together in NYC and had so much fun, and we were like, let's move here! Instead, she got off-track, dropped out of college and went to community college, and then just decided that she was going to work at her dad's company and hang out with her boyfriend. And she's like, 'It's so great! I love it!'" Amy explains with a heavy helping of disdain. "I keep trying to get her to move to New York, but she's not into it anymore." It's a weird feeling when all of a sudden your friend's dreams aren't the same as yours. Amy and her bestie still talk every day, but when it comes to achieving the dream, Amy has had to create her own squad of women who keep her moving forward. She relies on Kaylin, who is a reporter at a women's mag (with dreams of writing for the *New Yorker*) and knows how hard it is to maintain your dignity while being forced to dig up dirt on Rob Kardashian. Or she turns to Elizabeth, a friend from her hometown who graduated a few years earlier and landed a gig as the head of operations at a digital start-up with her eye on cashing in at the IPO. These chicks weren't there for the long high-school talks in Amy's bedroom, imagining what life would be like beyond their small sleepy town. But they're with her now, working through the labyrinth of how you get from where you are to where you ultimately want to be.

YOUR FAMILY IS YOUR FAMILY, AND THAT'S FINE

Just like you wish your best friends could share your vision of the Big Life, you also want the same kind of all-in enthusiasm from your family. But sometimes, their version of support doesn't fall in line with your idea of yourself.

Savannah still loves her side hustle as the editor-in-chief of the millennial website, but she scored a new day job in the music biz that let her ditch the bartending and marketing gigs. Plus, she seems to have finally pulled off the impossible: getting a cute, affordable apartment and a hot, supportive boyfriend. So it's hard to believe that not long ago, she was thinking of throwing in the towel on her big dream.

"I had no money, and I was tired of living with a 50-year-old guy whose name I got off of Craigslist," Savannah says. She was crawling the walls looking for a way out of her dark hole when an office manager job fell in her lap, a job that would have been soul-sucking, energy-draining drudgery—no matter how broke she was, she couldn't make herself do it. She'd made up her mind that she wanted to hold out for something that mattered when she made the mistake of telling her family. "My mom and sister wanted me to take the job," she says. "They didn't see other options. They thought it would be better to have a job that didn't interest me and to get paid, rather than hold out for a long shot that put me on the path to my dream," she says.

Having her mom and sister add their voices to the chorus of *no* she was hearing at every turn was painful. But big dreams need to be carefully guarded from doubters, and that meant pushing forward even though her family thought she was making a mistake. "My family believed in following a traditional, safe route, and it made me feel like I wasn't capable of doing anything outside of the norm," Savannah says. "Even now, they remind me of the astronomical odds of succeeding the way I want to."

With her family sitting on the sidelines of her most complex career questions, Savannah needed a deep bench of advisors—superambitious chicks she met at women's networking groups or through friends of friends—to help illuminate the path when things get really dark. One woman she turns to again and again is her business-side partner on the website, Marisa. They took some of the same classes in college and reconnected after graduation. That kind of shared history is even more valuable when every new opportunity makes you ask, "Is this right for me?"

ON YOUR OWN, BUT NOT ALONE

Grace, Amy, and Savannah are unlikely to ever cross paths. Grace loves the prestige and challenge of the C-suite. Savannah thrives off the edgy energy that comes with working in the music biz and on a shoestring start-up side hustle. Amy is establishing her own brand as a reporter.

The roads they're following are very different, but they share the same drive. Even as a teen, Grace had a long list of accomplishments she planned to tick off one by one: working for the UN, visiting Paris, working for one of the world's largest companies. Savannah's vision was more about skipping out of her small town, making a life in a big city, and finding a career that sings to the most creative parts of her being. Amy was driven by adventure.

But they are each desperate for connection—to know they're not alone.

And that's the true payoff of having a squad. It's validation of your deepest dreams. No matter how wildly ambitious, off-the-beaten path, or hard left turn your vision, the women you surround yourself with and who help you navigate the trickiest parts of building the Big Life are there to remind you that your dreams matter, that the path you're carving isn't impossible. They believe in you.

Make no mistake: Grace, Savannah, and Amy are proud of everything they've achieved on their own, but they didn't do it alone. They know that any of their accomplishments wouldn't have happened without the support they've gotten from the women who had their backs every step of the way.

"I've met other people who now encourage and inspire me, which allows me to get even further," Savannah says. "For the first time, I feel like I can do it all, and I think that's largely due to my support system. I've really started to learn what I'm capable of and understand my potential. Now, I can't even imagine not exploring as much as possible."

THE BIG LIFE
CONVERSATION

JENNIFER HYMAN
Cofounder and CEO of Rent the Runway

HOW HER SQUAD IS HER SECRET TO SUCCESS—
AT WORK AND IN LIFE

I met Jennifer Hyman years ago through a friend of a friend at some cocktail party that has now faded into memory. But I do remember what she was wearing: a full-length, inky-blue men's trench, belted tight around the waist—so *cool*. Jenn (as she likes to be called) is the epitome of badass—she speaks with such confidence about things that matter, like love, self-worth, and friendship—and you can't help being drawn into her orbit. And it turns out that's no accident. Jenn thrives on collaboration, and wants you to feel the power of sisterhood too.

Ann: When you were 16 years old, growing up in New Rochelle, NY, looking out your bedroom window, what did you dream your life would be like?

Jenn: At 16, I thought that I would be doing something that was creative. I didn't know what that really meant at the time because I hadn't been exposed to that many creative jobs. I didn't understand what the word *entrepreneur* was. I didn't know any entrepreneurs. Then I thought, "Well, I'm clearly going to be married; I want to have a *huge* family." I come from a big family, so that's always been the most important thing in my life. I liked the idea of living in a "tribe" that consists of your friends, your family, and extended family. I'd have this open-door policy and constantly be surrounded by people I love. I imagined I would have a husband and kids, but I always had this notion that I'd develop these lifelong friends and we would spend our lives together. I've always been someone who has derived energy and happiness from being around other people. So, it's not just about being extroverted; it's more that I just love being in a group. I'm more relaxed when I'm in a group. I live off the chaos of putting all different kinds of personalities together.

And so, one of the first things I did when I had the beginnings of financial success from Rent the Runway was buy a summer house near the beach. And I've called it the Dream House, because every weekend, I invite groups of people out to the house, commune-style, to just be together. People can come with their kids, and everyone is just lying around, spending time with each other. In our world, where people are spending more time at work and are more and more scheduled, that time when you can feel relaxed and build meaningful connections with people isn't going to be a scheduled dinner on a Tuesday night after you've worked for 12 hours that day. The most interesting conversations come during those relaxing, spontaneous moments, like when it's four o'clock in the afternoon after you've come back from the beach and you're sitting on a couch, *exhausted.*

A: How is your philosophy about the tribe reflected in your business?

J: I've always had this belief that everything is better in a group, everything is better in a team. But what's been amazing since I've started Rent the Runway, and we've built the community of six million women who are our members and our customers, is that that philosophy has been reinforced to me through our customers. One in every five customers, after she rents an outfit, posts a photo of herself to our site and tells the story of the night she got engaged, the day she gave an important presentation at work, or the weekend she just spent at the beach and how she felt about herself and this incredible celebratory experience in her life. She also gives data on how the outfit fit her and what she would recommend in terms of other people wearing the garment. Why would she do that? The only incentive she has is to pay this forward so that another woman can have an incredible experience feeling self-confident or powerful or beautiful or sexy before her job interview or date or wedding she's attending. I've seen millions of customers do this for each other so that other women could feel great about themselves—that has been extremely powerful for me.

A: The Rent the Runway community is certainly important to business, but who are the people in your tribe?

J: They're friends who I've made throughout my life. There's a big group of friends from undergrad who I've kept in touch with forever. There are groups of friends from high school. There are people that I met when I first moved to New York City. There are people who helped me found and start Rent the Runway. And then my fiancé and his friends and family—people that he's brought into the tribe.

A: Congratulations on your engagement! You've been candid about calling off a previous engagement. What did you learn from that experience about what you need in a relationship?

J: One of the reasons I decided to call off an engagement and pursue a different type of marriage is that the relationship I was in wasn't bringing me the joy and happiness that I knew I deserved and really wanted for my life. I wanted that big love. I didn't want one component of my life—my career—to be amazing, but then not have that same amazingness in my family and love life. I took that risk and called off my wedding when I was 33 years old. And I think that a lot of people would have been too scared to do that because they would have thought, Well, am I going to meet someone in time to have kids? And I was like, I know I will meet someone who I am completely in love with and I'm going to have family life and kids—and I have to trust in that. I have to be as aggressive and ambitious in my personal life as I am in my career.

And here I am almost 3 years later, and I found the love of my life. I feel so confident in this person, and I'm laughing with him every day. I think that this ambitiousness around having a full and rich life has to exist across every single section of your life. Have as much faith in your personal life as you do in your career. I am much better as a leader right now and much better at my job at Rent the Runway because I am also really happy in my personal life. And I don't just mean in my relationship with my fiancé. I also mean in my relationships with my family and friends. If you don't have the same ambition for yourself across all these different parts of your life, you're not going to be as successful in any given component of it.

A: That's amazing! What is your advice for women who are worried that they won't meet a partner or won't have children?

J: The world has changed. There are more options available to women now. For example, if you know you want to have kids, you can freeze your eggs. You have no idea if you're going to meet your partner when you're 40 or when you're 23. So why not have your eggs frozen so that you don't feel pressured to marry the wrong person? And you can increase the size of the funnel of people you can date. When I was in my 20s, the only way I could

meet people to date was in real life. If you wanted to meet someone, you had to be out constantly and wait for some serendipity,
to meet the right person at the right party on the right night.
Now, if you want to find a relationship, you can use Bumble or
Tinder or Hinge and go on a date every single night of the week.
In some cases, it's easier than it's ever been for women to get the
relationships they want.

**A: I'm so impressed with the way you've given even
deeper meaning to Rent the Runway by creating an initiative, Project Entrepreneur, that helps women start their
own businesses. Why is that important to you?**

J: What I'm trying to do with Project Entrepreneur is create a
community of women who are paying it forward to women just a
few steps behind them on their entrepreneurial journeys. Jenny
[her business partner, Jennifer Fleiss] and I started our business
7 years ago, so we've had so much time to learn. And often, it's not
very useful to receive advice from someone who is so far ahead of
you. I've been introduced to people who run companies with millions of customers, when we had like a hundred customers. And
it's not helpful to get advice from someone who is so far away from
the problems that you are having in the early days. You just want
someone who remembers the pain and the excitement and the
wildness of being in that same early position and who actually has
tactical feedback for you and tangible advice that you can turn
into an action plan.

It's very easy to give advice. I can go on television, I could
write a book, I could give all of these women advice on how they
should build their businesses and start their entrepreneurial
journeys. But it's a very, very different thing to sit down with a
woman who is a year into building her business and help her
draft a fundraising presentation for her Series A. Or make a
phone call on behalf of another entrepreneur to help her sell to
her first client. I think that in order to truly help others, a mentor needs to do some work on behalf of the mentee.

A: Your business is booming, you're able to give back to other entrepreneurs, you're getting married—does it feel like you "have it all?"

J: For this new generation of millennial women, having it all is certainly not going to look like what their mothers' "having it all" looked like. It's going to be in a different order. They might have kids before they're married. They might be in five different relationships before they find the right one. They might have five different types of careers. There's no one path, and what they love about that is this richness of doing a lot of things and being involved in the world in a more present way.

I want the big love. I want to change the way that women live. I want to inspire more women to become entrepreneurs. And I want to give back to my parents, family, and friends and do something important in the community—and I believe I can do all of those things.

6

EMBRACE YOUR MESS

WHY PILES OF DIRTY LAUNDRY, AN EMPTY FRIDGE, AND A FOUR-ESPRESSO-A-DAY HABIT ARE ACTUALLY SIGNS YOU'RE MAKING IT

One of the most amazing parts of my Big Life is that I get invited to talk to groups of young women about how they can get started in their careers and craft their own versions of the Big Life. I can spend all day on Twitter, Facebook, and Instagram, but it's so much better to be in a room full of Badass Babes, feel their energy, and make *real* connections. Sometimes, the conversation is very nuts and bolts about what kind of internship to apply for in college or how to get your résumé noticed in a massive pile of those from other job-seekers. Sometimes, people want me to tell my *Seventeen* stories, like about the time I met Justin Bieber when he was a bratty newbie; or the first sit-down I had with Taylor Swift, who came to my office with thick black eyeliner and tight spiral curls, and we ended up talking about where she should go shopping; or when I accidentally touched Beyoncé's butt while we were posing for photographs. If I'm lucky, the conversation moves toward hopes and dreams and the nagging fears that hold you back from putting your most awesome self out there in the world. That's oxygen to me.

But there's one question I get over and over, and I'm still stunned by it. Inevitably, someone raises her hand and asks, "How do we handle work-life balance?" The room gets quiet, like I'm about to reveal a giant secret that's the key to perfectly balancing work with life. Are you ready for the answer? Work-life balance is a sham. It doesn't exist. And I don't think it should. Frankly, I don't even get why you are asking. Are you worried about how you'll balance kids and work now when you're still swiping left on 99 percent of the dudes on your Tinder? At this moment in your life, it's your job to work as hard as you can and explore as much as you can so you can figure out the best expression of your awesomeness in the world. Now is not the time to be worried about how you'll navigate school pickup when you're on deadline for a big project.

Work-life balance is a sham. It doesn't exist.

This is not to say that your life won't get exponentially more complicated when you decide to start a family. It will, undoubtedly. And that's when, in conversation with your partner, you'll need to make a plan. But there's no sense worrying about that moment until it comes. When it comes, I promise, you will work it out.

For you right now, there is no point when work ends and life begins. It's all work all the time, and all life all the time. You want what you do for a living to feel like actual living. That's the magic trick. It's not like you're going into some secret chamber of work and grinding it out for 8 hours until you're set free on the other side, where your real life picks up again. It's a huge myth that our days should be perfectly compartmentalized like a bento box special. Gone are the times when work, friends, family, and fun all fit into their own designated slots. You're easily clocking 50-plus hours a week at work. Who isn't? And when you do eventually leave the office to hit a spin class or a happy-hour networking event, it's not unusual for you to check your email nonstop to see if anyone responded to your outline of next steps on a big project. After a dinner of take-out noodles—holding chopsticks in one hand and swiping through Snapchat stories with the other—you'll kick aside the growing pile of laundry and settle in with your laptop to do some work on the side gig you took on. And when you do go out, you're not going to leave the party early just because you have an 8:30 breakfast meeting. Instead, you'll upgrade to a venti with an extra shot of espresso at Starbucks in the morning so you won't have to miss the fun (or networking ops). Side hustles, charity runs, volunteering, networking events—you want to do it all, and you should. Say yes to everything.

And yet, I'm very aware of that feeling that there's so much to do and not enough time to do it. That's real. It's not pleasant to suspect that opportunities are slipping through your fingers. But the more you try to bring balance to your life, like it's some kind of Marie Kondo life-changing tidying-up magic, the more you're in danger of creating anxiety that's only going to magnify the mess, rather than harness it to create opportunities. You have to embrace the mess.

WHEN THE MESS IS THE KEY TO SUCCESS

I used to work for a woman whose desk was the messiest nightmare of Post-Its, memos, newspapers, files, and tubes of lip gloss. It was literally layers of stuff on top of other stuff. I am a piler and not a filer, so I'm comfortable with a lot of clutter, but her mess was beyond the pale. It gave me the willies, frankly. Still, she knew exactly where everything was at all times. We'd stop in the middle of a meeting for her to rifle around, looking for a sliver of paper she'd written some important thought on . . . and she'd find it every time. This woman not only embraced her mess, she thrived on it. She loved the clutter because she knew that mess contained creative brilliance, and to try to wrestle it into place would kill her mojo.

WHEN THE MESS IS YOUR MOJO

Sitting across from Jordan in a Greenwich Village gastropub as she sips whiskey from a heavy crystal glass, I see no outward signs of mess. Even her drink is neat. She says, "I sat next to a cute guy on my first business-class flight, and he told me it was hotter to order it this way." Jordan tucks a glossy black curl behind her ear and leans forward to show me her Trello board. Lit up in vibrant shades of purple, green, and yellow are all her work projects, side projects, performances, writing deadlines, podcasts, board meetings, and SoulCycle appointments—the deadlines and commitments seem overwhelming. But Jordan quickly lets me know that she stays as busy as she can handle, and she handles *a lot*. There's always room for more—another project, commitment, activity, or performance is just a quick tap away on Trello. "I have boards for everything," she says as she flicks one finished task over to the "done" column. Jordan is beyond busy, and she says that's the key to

JORDAN'S MESS-MANAGEMENT SECRETS

"I use Trello to organize projects. It's easy, does a million things, and you can share it with other people working on the same project. I'm also sure to block out sections of time for exercise, doctor appointments, and even dating. If I get a last-minute after-work invite, I'm not going to let day-four greasy bedhead keep me from going. I'll just breeze past the front desk of SoulCycle on my way to the locker room and act like I'm on my way to change for a class. They have the best shampoo and killer blow dryers! I've also learned that I need 6-plus hours of sleep—otherwise I'm a crying mess."

her success. "I feel like I'm always one deliverable from drop-ping everything. But I'm the most productive when it's almost all falling apart. If I'm not nearly falling apart, I'm only going to deliver a B+." Jordan is a Badass Babe who will settle for nothing less than an A+ life, and why not?

With every new task she takes on, Jordan proves to her-self that she can do more. "I don't say no," she explains. This can-do-more attitude has been ingrained in her since she was a child. "My grandmother always told me that if you're asked to do something, and you can do it, it's your obligation to do so. She believed it was selfish to say no if you can help."

But there was a time when being the can-do chick didn't exactly ingratiate her with the other girls. "In middle school, I was the girl who ate lunch with teachers and read Nancy Drew books in the bathroom," Jordan says. But that social iso-lation gave her a few extra blank spots on her calendar that she filled by practicing filling out her college applications—starting when she was 12. Big dreams for ambitious girls flourish in quiet places. It was while in the pressure-cooker of a prestigious college that Jordan started to see that always pushing herself to the max was how to make the magic hap-pen. "I worked three jobs in college and took 23 credits every semester. I was also in four organizations, theater pro-ductions, and a band. I was at it every day from 8:00 a.m. to 1:00 a.m. Junior year, I laid out all my syllabi and every single performance and due date. I got nervous when I realized that there were only 4 days in the entire semester when some-thing wasn't due. I knew it wasn't sustainable. I was drinking a 12-pack of Diet Coke every day, and I remember having a middle-of-the-night breakdown in a booth at an IHOP while drinking the bottomless coffee. But here's the thing: It was my best semester ever. I got a 4.0." Jordan set up an endurance test for herself and found that, as with diamonds, the pressure made her stronger and more valuable.

It's hard to tinker with anyone's personal brand of success. I have used a Pilot Razor Point blue pen ever since my first job out of college, because my tough-as-nails boss used that brand of pen. And if you took them away from me, I'm convinced my ideas would be a bit more pedestrian. I'm sure you have your own magic formula. And so, for Jordan, once the overly caffeinated panic faded, those busy-all-the-time habits endured. Jordan is still actively pushing herself to the brink as if she has something to prove—if not to her clients, then to herself. "Last November, I had everything big due—a speech, a midterm for grad school, a work project—and it was really crazy," she says. "I left directly from my exam to the airport, where I got on a flight to go to Boston. I was giving a speech at Harvard that afternoon." Plus, it was her birthday. Oh, and there was a guy who shoehorned himself into her schedule too. "The only way my boyfriend and I could be together was for him to fly up to Boston to take me to dinner."

Jordan wouldn't know how to create work-life balance even if it were a project on her Trello board. For women like Jordan, recharging their batteries with a peaceful beach vacation or a daily meditation practice is *not* going to make them more productive. For Jordan, more is more; and she isn't in denial that all these commitments have her dangling dangerously close to the edge.

And frankly, there have been times she's slipped over that edge.

Her first venture after business school was a buzzy dotcom that she built from the ground up. After a splashy launch party in a fancy New York City hotel and being featured in just about every big paper and women's mag, the business couldn't raise the funding it needed to continue growing, and it shut down. Jordan found herself dealing with a major failure for the first time. For the chick who was president of every club, got straight As, and kicked ass at every job she'd had, this was a major blow. Exhausted and emotionally drained, she took to her bed for *a month* to let herself heal and re-energize. And this was not a one-time occurrence. Jordan says she hits a crisis point every few months, but she's learned to look out for it, deal with it, and get herself quickly back into action. "If I'm not feeling in control, I get on the couch and *cry*. Sometimes, I have to cancel everything for 2 or 3 days until I can get my equilibrium." The crying is a regular release, and then she gets back up.

But frankly, it's not the size of Jordan's mess that scares her, or that the more she takes on, the closer she is to dropping something. She has taken on *more* than she can handle and proven to herself that she can survive—and that's what keeps her filling all those blank spots on her calendar, daring herself to see how much she can achieve. And if you're one of those women like Jordan, the only way forward is to generate an even bigger mess and see what magic you can make out of it.

THE MESS THAT DRIVES YOU AWAY FROM YOUR DREAM

As much as you want to carve your own path, the pressure to get on a track and stay there is all around. It's baked into the college-prep classes you take in high school. You then feel obligated to choose a major based on the number of credits you've accumulated (even if it was the one rando elective in freshman year that sparked your passion). Then there's the promise of promotions in your first on-the-job training sessions. But what happens when that track is steering you away from what makes you happy rather than closer to it? Life can get messy when you're not following your heart.

Sydney loved fashion so much that, as a teen, she was styling her friends and staging her own runway shows in her backyard. But pursuing a career in fashion didn't feel "serious enough," she explains. "I felt I had to lock those feelings down and get on the Achievement Train so I could get into a good college."

Sydney, now 31, is bubbly and charming, with a huge white smile and perfect bright lipstick. And yet I get a few glimpses into the messy corners of her life: emails time-stamped at 3:30 a.m., meetings that get rescheduled at the last minute, long periods of radio silence. When she breezes into a local café to meet me, she's a half-hour late, and she doesn't bother with an explanation, just a big hug. It's hard to criticize her for being irresponsible or rude because she's so genuine and focused in person that all the mess fades into the background. Her enthusiasm and warmth are contagious, and it's no surprise when she reveals that she was the activities director of her sorority in the early 2000s. "I went back and forth from the library to parties in my Juicy Couture track suit!" she confesses. (Don't judge: You had that track suit too. I even had that track suit!) During summers, she loved selling clothes at a department store. "I was in the top three sellers," she says, still proud of her accomplishment. But that led her to a postcollege career in corporate sales, not fashion. The goal-oriented culture in the corporate sales department inspired her. "I told my parents I would make

$100,000 during the first year in my job. They thought I couldn't do it," she says with a broad smile. "I made $101,000."

From that point on, Sydney's journey on the Achievement Train sped up. She kept a long list above her desk of the number of calls she had to make, the number of new clients she had to bring in. Next to her list was a picture of what she wanted to do with the bonuses she'd earn: helicopter lessons and trips to Paris. She didn't want to splurge on designer handbags; she wanted experiences that would feed her soul. "I was quickly doing really well and soon was making over $300,000 a year. I went from meeting to meeting to meeting with a big bag of binders and business cards. I had a $5,000-a-month expense account and was eating at the best restaurants every night." What's not to love, right? Well, there's a classic saying that success is noisy—friends calling, glasses clinking, new opportunities to talk about . . . Sydney had the volume turned up to 11. And failure, the saying goes, is silent—no one calls, your calendar is empty, there's nothing to toast. You'd do anything to keep the noise of success going. But it's in those quiet moments that you can hear your own voice. And Sydney's inner voice kept interrupting the din of her success to let her know the Achievement Train she'd been on had taken her away from her real dream: fashion.

Glimpses of Sydney's creative self had started to peek through her serious business exterior. She designed a few party dresses that she trotted out at after-hours work events and loved the feedback she got from other women who were stuck in a Banana Republic rut. She found herself pushing aside the business books on her bookshelf to make room for tons of fashion books and even spiritual books. She'd revisit one in particular again and again: The Alchemist, which is, at its core, about the power of listening to your heart.

Sydney had begun listening, and in one bright and shining moment, she knew she needed a radical change. On her 26th birthday, she had a party in her apartment. The champagne was chilled, and there were loads of guests, but all of them were clients; none were friends. "That's when I realized that being a great businessperson was important, but it didn't make me *happy.*"

And so late one night, desperate for a new plan, she Googled "fashion school," signed up for a semester, and packed her bags. She hadn't even given notice at her job yet, but this was her way of making a promise to herself that she couldn't break. This was the experience that all those bonus checks had really been for after all. She hadn't fully realized that she'd been building a "fuck off" fund—a secret stash of money that gives you the financial freedom to leave a bad job or a destructive relationship, or, as was the case with Sydney, make a hard right turn in your career. But with every step she took away from the sales gig, she felt stronger, more confident, and more like herself.

Sydney has never regretted leaving her incredibly lucrative job in advertising sales to be an entrepreneur. The mess is still there—it's even messier when you're building a business from the ground floor. But this time,

---

TIPS FROM CHICKS
AT THE TABLE

SYDNEY'S MESS-MANAGEMENT SECRETS

"Working in the fashion business is incredibly tough—it's exhausting. But whenever I feel like walking away, I look at a folder I keep in my inbox called Lovely. It has hundreds of emails in it now from people who have told me that my designs made them feel beautiful. That reminds me that there is no way I can stop."

the mess is propelling her down the right path rather than pulling her away from it. "I've made my work what I want my life to be. It didn't used to be like that. My life was not *fun* in sales. It looked glamorous and sexy and amazing from the outside, but it wasn't fulfilling," she says. "It's superhard, but I know I'm working toward something greater, and that's what drives me." Sydney found the sweet spot where what you do for a living feels like actual *living*.

WHEN IGNORING YOUR DREAM MAKES A BIGGER MESS

We talk so much about honoring your dream, but actually following it is hard, isn't it? There are so many real-world considerations: money, access to resources, training, support.

And then there are the sneaky ways we sabotage our dreams: fear of failure, fear of success, complicated ideas about who you're supposed to be that are nearly impossible to untangle from who you *want* to be.

Nothing feels worse than waking up at 3:00 a.m. with that vision of what you want to be demanding your attention. It's not like your dream is going to politely knock on your door, asking nicely for you to come out and notice her. The more you suppress that dream, the louder she's going to bang—and the bigger your mess is going to be.

One of my favorite experiences I had while working on this book was receiving a note from a Badass Babe who found a way to honor her dream. Jessica had an important job working in finance at a big corporation. She received amazing training and was engaged in challenging projects, but it wasn't satisfying and she didn't know how to change direction to something that felt more in tune with her true self. "I'm almost 30. I feel like I should be doing something or working toward something that I actually have a passion for," Jessica says. She'd been on the fast track . . . but it felt like the fast track to nowhere. "Two years ago, I was traveling 70 percent of the time. I was in Asia or Europe, and I was like, holy shit, I'm 25 and single. I'm missing out on engagement parties; I'm missing out on things that are very important to me. And I started to feel not successful." This is the kind of situation that causes a Badass Babe to feel a trickle of dread on Sunday morning that shifts to full-fledged Sunday Scaries come evening.

Jessica asked to be transferred to another department in her company that would give her more free time so she could focus more on her personal life. But it wasn't enough, and over a dinner at my place, listening to the stories of other women who were squeezing their passion projects into full, messy lives, she knew she had to make a bigger change. After the dinner, she wrote me a note: "I am starting a new job in a few weeks to follow my dream of being a CFO at a not-for-profit!"

Jessica saw no need to toss all her achievements aside to honor her dream; she just needed to shift over to a place where her skills and passion to make a difference could happily coexist.

WHEN THE MESS IS INSTITUTIONALIZED

When I first came to *Seventeen* as the new editor-in-chief, I inherited an office culture where everyone stayed really late. I assumed that people were working on stories or writing pitch memos. Everyone would order dinner and take cabs home after an incredibly long day. Then, they'd do it again the next day, just slightly more drained than the day before. But when I took a good look at the workflow, I realized it didn't have to be that way. And I started to see that people were staying late to impress me or as some weird badge of honor. No one does great work at the end of a 14-hour shift. And so we reworked the system so the late nights didn't have to happen so often.

It takes a team to put together a magazine, and there was no changing the fact that the stories had to go from writer to editor, maybe back to the writer, to me, to the copy editors, to the art department, and so on. It's not like you can just break a system. But we worked hard together to figure out how to do it in a way that got everyone out the door by 7:00 p.m. The point is that office culture isn't always healthy, and it's not always the way it has to be forever and ever. It sucks if the one at the top doesn't see it this way, and I've been there. I've had the capricious bosses. I've been the girl sleeping under the conference table, and I know what it's like to edit copy at midnight. That's why, when I came to *Seventeen*, I knew that the decisions I made would make life either hellish or bearable for my team.

Not everyone has a team of execs who are willing to morph how they work to make life better for their employees. And as much as we all want a job that allows us flexible schedules, less face time at the office, and fewer meetings, there are plenty of jobs where that isn't even a remote possibility. Doctors, lawyers, investment bankers—these are just a few of the professions that are so lockstep and hierarchical that it would be front-page news if they made even the tiniest tweak to their inscrutable cultures. And yet, the young women who enter those fields now often still have the same yearning for freedom from the grind. And so what do you do when you're stuck in a system that couldn't care less about what you're yearning for? Six associates at one of the most prestigious law firms in the country gathered around my dining room table to discuss this at one of my Badass Babe dinners.

Avery, 29, never meant to be a lawyer. "When I was 16, I thought I wanted a family—I didn't want to work. And then when my dad lost his job in the recession and my family was incredibly unstable, I was like, 'All I want is stability,'" she explains. "And that's why I went to law school—to provide, bottom line."

The six-figure salary that comes as a fourth-year associate has helped soothe her money anxiety. But the usurious 8 percent interest on her student loans and the 12-hour days that run until 10:00 p.m. leave her zero time to enjoy it. "I make enough money that I no longer have to drink rail vodka," adds Jennifer, 30, another associate in her class, who also admits that she entered the law firm's lockstep system because she felt pressured to take care of her family financially. "So, now I can afford Grey Goose—when I leave work at midnight on a Friday."

This group of lawyers bonds over gallows humor about the brutal grind of their jobs.

"Someone I work with told me she threw up this morning because she was so stressed," says Francesca, 31, a French ex-pat. "She forgot a comma," she joked.

"I feel like I constantly have to make choices. Do I work or sleep? Do I work and go to the gym and skip sleep? What if I want to watch TV? When do I date?" says Emma, 30, who wishes someone could give her more hours in the day. "I'm constantly making decisions about what to sacrifice and what to *actually do*."

And even though each of the women at the table says they like their work—they feel smart, engaged—they hate having no control over the brutal grind of long days.

"When I was growing up, I always thought I was going to do something great," explains Melissa, 31. "But now it's like, even if I succeeded at the highest level at the law firm, who cares? It's not that great."

What do you do when you're stuck in a system that couldn't care less about what you're yearning for?

Avery knew it was time to address the mess when she started dreaming that she was sending emails in her sleep. "I'm not an anxious person, but I found myself dreaming about my work—as in *nightmaring* about my work," she says. The stress of Avery's job reached such an intense level that she actually thought she was doing work while she was sleeping—it didn't feel like a dream. It felt real. "I was constantly having phantom emails, entire deals, entire transactions—all the details that go with it happening in my dream. You wake up, go to your computer, and look for the emails you think you sent, sit in front of it, and you're really confused. And if somebody is in bed with you, they're like, what the fuck are you doing? This was actually making me a worse lawyer—and I just thought I needed to stop. I was making myself miserable and the people around me miserable."

Avery is the envy of some of her law-firm pals because she managed to trade in the stress of her law-firm job for a job in the legal department of a company with better hours and the same pay. "The pace is much better; I still do exactly the same work. It's not the expectation that you work past 7:00 p.m. or on weekends. It has allowed my anxiety to chill out a little bit."

It's a plan B that allows her to do high-level, satisfying work and reclaim some of her life. Most of the women around my table that night have something else brewing on the horizon that will lift them out of the brutal grind. One wants to shift into the vegan-food industry, and another wants to do government policy work.

Only a few think they'll stick it out to make partner at the firm, but they all agree that the excellence demanded of them is shaping them for something bigger and better down the line. Sometimes, knowing that you're aiming for something more meaningful makes the necessary mess more manageable for now.

WHEN NOT TO EMBRACE THE MESS

I've heard some crazy stories of dysfunctional workplaces: predator bosses, toxic coworkers, institutionalized sexism, life-destroying workloads. There was the assistant at a travel company who dodged her boss's drunken pass at an after-hours work event and found herself sidelined into running his personal errands. There was the junior account exec who was asked to cover up some financial monkey business. There was the advertising designer who felt she was actively being sabotaged by the older women in the firm who were protecting their turf. There is no embracing that mess. You have to protect your heart and soul and get out of there ASAP. Keep a paper trail. File complaints with human resources, and if your safety is in danger, call the police.

SO LONG, BALANCE— HELLO, INTEGRATION

I've been that young editor who went to every networking event, chased every party, said yes to every invite. And frankly, that's still how I operate. I hate to feel like I'm missing out! And I've found that what keeps it all from dissolving from mess into massive chaos is that now all my stuff goes together. Almost everything I say yes to is helping young women be awesome in the world. I'm on the board of a nonprofit that helps women in the South Bronx get their GEDs so they can go to college. I'm advising a social-good start-up that helps young women in developing countries go to school. I'm devoted to a small women-entrepreneurs networking group. I say yes to dinners and cocktails with a few women's media organizations. I even try to make working out into an opportunity to deepen the relationships with a few women I admire; we'll meet up at a Pilates or boot camp class. (After all, too many happy hours swilling sauvignon blanc doesn't help the mess. I can't embrace anything with a hangover.)

THE BIG PICTURE IS PRETTIER

There comes a time when you can sense your focus being pulled away from the things that truly matter, and you have to accept that you can't do everything.

Eventually, you need to start delegating. No one should ever have to feel weird about asking for help, no matter what it is—whether this means giving yourself permission to drop off your laundry, order groceries, use a cleaning service, or hire a full-time nanny. Life is full of pesky tasks and important duties. But you have the power to decide what you will handle and what you will delegate to someone else. No guilt. Once these items are automatically being handled, your focus will shift back to where it's supposed to be.

It's hard to imagine all the different strands of your Big Life prettily tied together. Right now, when you look at your life, what you're seeing is a mess, and that's okay. There's no magical moment when life suddenly becomes all smooth sailing. The mess will always be there, and you'll never be able to tackle it all. But when you give yourself permission to let it go, it becomes background noise. As your dreams become closer and more booming, soon you won't hear the noise at all.

EMBRACE-THE-MESS LIFE HACKS

My Hack: The Weekly Blow-Dry

I'm a huge fan of a weekly blow-dry. Get a regular early-Monday appointment (if you can get a polish change at the same time, all the better), and with a little dry shampoo and a curling iron, you can make the blow-dry last all week. Without the professional blowout, it would take me 40 minutes a day to wash, blow-dry, and curl my hair. That's 40 minutes more I have to get a little extra work done, squeeze in a quickie meeting, or even have morning coffee with my husband!

Nicole's Hack: Divvy Up the Cost of a Cleaner

Cleaning an apartment shared by three women takes time—and being annoyed with your roomies for not doing their share of housework takes way too much energy. While it wasn't in my personal budget to pay for a cleaner, I realized that if you call one of these new cleaning services like Handy, and divide it by three, it's not much at all. Chances are your roommates will readily agree to this. You'll save loads of time not having to deal with drudge work . . . not to mention the drama of living with messy chicks.

Emily's Hack: Train Together

I work *a lot*, and the first thing I want to let slip is exercise. Sometimes, it felt like I was exercising instead of meeting friends, and that was a bummer. Or, I was seeing people but not exercising—and feeling like crap about it. The solution was a fun run. A few of my friends and I decided to do a charity 5K together. We trained for a few weeks before the race. We were able to catch up and exercise. Now we're taking things up a notch and training for a half-marathon.

Clarissa's Hack: Outsource

I place a weekly order of my favorite foods from Fresh Direct. I keep crucial items like coffee and almond milk on my recurring order so that I never run out. It saves me time, and it also helps ensure that I have healthy food around. I always have something to eat for breakfast and dinner so I'm not always ordering out. If I'm really strapped for time, I'll pay for my laundry to be done too.

Margot's Hack: Reign It In

I've learned to notice the signs of when my life is getting out-of-control messy. If I'm not returning texts and emails from friends or family, or I'm staying up until after midnight working, I'm on the verge of getting out of control. When that happens, I make a point of prioritizing my work, focusing on what needs to get done right away, and making a plan. That might mean seeing if another team member is available to help me knock out a project or getting an intern to take over the minor tasks.

THE BIG LIFE
CONVERSATION

ALEXA VON TOBEL
Founder and CEO of LearnVest

HOW HER MESS MADE HER MILLIONS

When Alexa von Tobel sold LearnVest, her 6-year-old financial-planning service aimed at millennials, for more than $250 million, the entire financial services industry gasped. But von Tobel was no dilettante. She felt that financial services were ready for some "youthful disruption," so, in 2009, at age 25, she dropped out of Harvard Business School (never mind the recession) to focus on her dream of making managing money as easy as downloading a song. The fact that she had a baby the same year she sold her company only adds to her badass-ness.

Ann: I've never met a successful woman who couldn't pinpoint the dream she had for herself at 16 years old. What was yours?

Alexa: When I was 16 years old, it was so clear to me. I felt like I could do *anything*. In my book *Financially Fearless*, the dedication to my parents reads, "To my mom and dad—for allowing me to believe in my wildest dreams and not for a moment letting on that they were wild." When I was 16, my vision of the future was that I was going to have a very robust, very full career in business. CEOs had always been my version of rock stars. I was always more interested in what the CEO of Coca-Cola was doing than what Madonna was doing.

AS: You clearly have no problem dreaming big, and yet no matter how much confidence you have in your vision for yourself, there are so many forces in the world that try to diminish your dreams, or put up roadblocks, or tell you to sit still and wait for the promotion or the title or the raise. How do you deal with that?

AVT: You have to just be unwilling to take no for an answer. Not in a confrontational way, but I'll say, okay, let's think out of the box. What if we go this way? What if we go this other route? I'd find creative ways around those roadblocks so they weren't roadblocks; they became *opportunities*. I really do believe it's all in how you view things. I sat with an entrepreneur recently, and her idea was to start a small law firm. And I was like, why can't it be a big law firm? Dream bigger than you would have dreamed originally. It just means stretching a bit beyond what your original premise was. Then I said, "Why can't you be a Supreme Court justice?" And she was like, "Well, no one ever said that I was allowed to." Why does someone have to say that you're allowed to? And I think it's just reframing your own ambition. Which doesn't mean you'll end up being a Supreme Court justice, but it does mean you'll go further than if you had that small ambition.

You can't boil the ocean, but you should at least *want* to. Shoot for the moon, land among the stars—it is that basic. If you're only trying to run a mile, you may only run a half-mile.

But if you try to run a marathon, you may run 10 miles. That's the kind of perspective with which I want people to approach life. And that doesn't mean I haven't been told no, and I haven't been punched in the face, and I haven't been pushed down. I'm just unwilling to view those as roadblocks. I'm just totally unwilling to view those as negative.

AS: It can be hard to bulldoze past all the roadblocks though. What are the nos that have stuck with you?

AVT: When I was getting my seed funding for LearnVest, I was dropping out of business school and just trying to get something up. I was literally duct-taping things together. People were like, "Come back to me when you have this, or come back to me when you have that." I thought, okay! That is not a no! I'll be back to you in 30 days. A lot of it comes down to being likable. I'll make you laugh, and I'll be back!

AS: I've heard you talk about those early days with people working in your living room. You made them dinner to encourage them to keep going. You must have been busy, overwhelmed, and exhausted. How did you get through those days?

AVT: I'm really comfortable with the unknown. I'm comfortable with uncertainty. I'm comfortable with risk. I'm embracing the journey. I'm not sitting here aggressively focused on the outcome. I'm focused on today and making sure that today can actually be enjoyable too. I'll give you an example. I was planning a party with a friend. We got some snacks, we got some drinks, we got some plates. And I'm like, okay, we've got all the things we need, and we'll show up with great attitudes, and it's going to be a fun party! And my friend, meanwhile, was like, we don't have the details for the recipes, we don't have the details of the drinks, we don't have the details of how the ice is going to get made. And I remember looking at her and saying, "But we have all the ingredients for success. We're good."

I am very detail-oriented, but that shows my tolerance for not having everything perfect while being certain that the outcome is going to be successful.

AS: Do you need to know the end goal in order for the mess to be okay?

AVT: Yes, I do need to know where I'm going. I know where my North Pole is; I know exactly what I'm running toward. I think most people have a deep intuition of what they hope life will look like.

AS: Now that you're beyond the days of having people crash in your living room, how do you keep yourself centered and motivated?

AVT: I go to the gym 5 days a week, and I make sure to get a lot of sleep. At the gym, it's about sheer sweat. After 6 minutes of sweating, you can feel the positive endorphins kick in. When I have about 20 minutes of that kind of sweating, I'm so much more capable of taking on more things.

AS: You had a baby the same week you sold your company. That seems like a pretty monumental mess to have to handle all at once. So often, I hear from women that they can't imagine navigating a big career and having a baby.

AVT: Forget about it being a baby. Life throws so much stuff at you. It throws illnesses at you, it throws parent illnesses at you, it throws sibling hardships. Having a child is such an invaluable life milestone, but I see it as any other event in your life. You can't plan for the unexpected. You can try to plan for a child all you want, but you don't know what that's going to look like. You don't know if you'll get pregnant easily, you don't know if you'll have twins . . . so it's better to have a life strategy that says you're going to roll with the punches when they come.

LearnVest got acquired on a Wednesday, and I went into labor on Sunday. I couldn't have planned for that. I had no control over that. Perfect plans get blown up and thrown out the window every day. You're better off relying on being agile than on plans, creating an infrastructure for when things do go wrong, and being comfortable with the unexpected. Life is uncertain, and the more you get comfortable with knowing that, the more skilled you are at tackling the realities of life.

7
THE JOURNEY MATTERS

YOU CAN'T FAST-FORWARD TO THE SPOILS

I hate to even say that you're on a "journey." It sounds like an inspirational poster, doesn't it? After all, it's your *life*—you're living it every day. But the truth is, the journey matters. No matter how clear your vision of where you want to be—or even if you have no vision at all right now—it's all the micro steps you're taking that prepare you to make your future your own. A path that leads straight to piles of money, industry respect, fawning profiles, legions of fans, and unconditional love might sound nice. But a truly epic journey is characterized by surprise twists and unforgettable characters that help make your ideas richer, smarter, and more interesting.

You want your story to be *Odyssey*-worthy!

Over pizza on a hot June night, Emily gives the SparkNotes of her journey: She was obsessed with the movie *Almost Famous* as a teen, so she went to college to study music journalism. Turns out she didn't like asking nosy questions, so she took a gap year and snagged a gig as the assistant (and sometimes babysitter) for a literary agent. She went back to school to finish her degree in film and PR and found a new fire to be a film producer. After some early, heady success with a video team, she couldn't find any other production work, and so she took the closest thing she could get: an administrative job at a talent agency.

"I'm really happy to be a little fish in a big pond—I'm just happy to be in the pond. But I'm suddenly terrified that I'm never going to get where I want to go," she says.

Then, she quietly confides the one thing that everyone else around the table is thinking: "All the pain and suffering is fine, just as long as it's *worth* it." She smiles at the other chicks nodding in agreement. I suspect you're nodding too. Emily is excited about her job but worried that there's zero opportunity for growth. She's last in a long queue of equally ambitious young women vying for a chance to make their mark. And while Emily is dating, she can't help wondering when she's going to connect with the right person, or *any* person. "I've lost track of how many people I've dated in the last year. I'm the queen of the first date! But rarely do I go on a second," she admits.

Emily's anxiety stems from not knowing what's going to come next. She just wants to believe that her early job experiences and string of Tinder dates will lead her to something meaningful. No one wants to be stuck wondering how the mind-numbing entry-level job or countless temp assignments will get you out of the zone where you're bringing PB&J to the office daily for lunch. It's not that you have to have blind faith that your future will magically be big and bright. But you do have to trust that everything you're doing *now* will make your future bigger and brighter.

INTRODUCING THE MACHINE

Sometimes you encounter a woman who is *so* sure of herself that it's next-level inspiring. She walks into the most intimidating meetings with self-possessed confidence. She's so authoritative when she speaks that you believe every single word. There's no hair twirling, nail biting, or nervous fiddling. She'd be intimidating if she weren't so warm and funny in a way that draws you in. How does she do it? That energy is 100-percent *experience*. She probably made every insecurity-inducing mistake along the way, and course-corrected again and again until she became the master of her domain. And you will get there too. But until you have, as Malcolm Gladwell says, 10,000 hours of expertise under your belt,

The Machine

It's the process that molds, shapes, polishes, buffs, and shines you to step into the spotlight of your own life. Once you've been through the Machine, you're smarter, stronger, and more capable, and every single person you meet can feel your confidence from across the room.

you still need to learn to project authority like the true Badass Babe you are. You want to be the woman whose message is heard.

How do you get there? By going through what I call the Machine. It's the process that molds, shapes, polishes, buffs, and shines you to step into the spotlight of your own life. Once you've been through the Machine, you're smarter, stronger, and more capable, and every single person you meet can sense your confidence from across the room. It's easiest to see the effect of the Machine in celebrities. Take Rihanna. The first time I met her was at a beauty conference at a large Florida convention center in the mid-2000s. She was a cute girl with honey blonde hair standing in the corner as beauty execs excitedly talked about her. I don't think she even said a word. She was practically hiding behind her manager's skirt—that's how shy she was. Pretty, but nothing about her said International Superstar.

Then, the Machine went to work. She found a signature music style, honed her IDGAF attitude, and crafted a bold public image that let us know this was not just another honey blonde mid-2000s pop star. First, her hair went jet-black and was cropped short. The makeup turned bold and experimental. Her clothes got tougher and tighter. And then came a daring nakedness that turned traditional pop stars' coquettish come-ons on their head: Her nudity was a freedom that said, I can be nearly naked on the red carpet, in front of hundreds of cameras, and not care what you think about it. Rihanna wanted you to look and then let you know that this was not a show for you—this was an expression of who she was as a person and as an artist. That's the Machine at work on its highest levels. Shaping who you want to become, shaping what you want to say about yourself, and refining the image you want to project to the world. And frankly, shaping how you see yourself too. The Machine helped Rihanna go from shy to superstar—not just on the outside but the inside as well.

It's the same type of power you feel when you're wearing 4-inch stilettos: You stand taller; you take up more room; you are more commanding. And even if you aren't feeling all that commanding at first, other people see you that way and treat you as if you are!

It's never about the shoes though. This is about creating an outward reflection that matches the wonderful things you have going on inside. It's about making your public image boost your *self*-image, and vice versa. We all put ourselves through a version of the Machine so that we're projecting an image that says we're smart or strong or clever or creative—or whatever we want to be seen as—and it makes us believe that we are all those things too.

SOMETIMES THE MACHINE HAPPENS TO YOU

Remember how terrified you were the first time you had to give a presentation during a meeting? You might have stumbled a bit, said the wrong thing, or botched the computer link-up to the big conference room screen while everyone waited with annoyed glances at the clock. But you got through it, and you probably made a few mental notes to yourself about what not to do next time (for one, get to the conference room early and check the computer connection *before* you start the meeting). Each presentation ended with you getting better at it—and feeling more ready for the next round. You slowly but surely learned how to navigate your way through that process. Every scary thing that you've gotten better at—

(continued on page 140)

ASK A
Badass Babe

HOW TO MASTER THE MACHINE

Carmen Lilly is one of those Badass Babes who is so impressive and warm that just being in her orbit makes you feel prettier, cooler, and taller! She's a former shopgirl turned stylist (with a training in classical art!) who gave Rihanna her original street style. Now, she's dedicating her styling work to "empowering women who empower others." The goal in crafting your image and filling out your wardrobe, she says, is so you can feel confident and "focus on the work, not on what you're wearing." Amen, sister! Here's her advice to help you craft a look that lets the world know you mean business.

Refine your message.

In college, it was fine to have a uniform of sweatshirts and leggings— it said you were busy studying/napping/working out. And then for your internship or first job, you probably disguised all personality in some generic pencil skirt and simple blouse situation. That worked too, since you were there to learn—and frankly, you were making so little money that a couple of interchangeable pieces were all you could afford. But once you start to get a sense of your possibility at work, you want your look to match your message. Do you want your bosses to think you are smart, focused, creative, bubbly, bold, or serious? Your clothes have to help carry that message. Fill up the dressing room—or better yet, order a ton of stuff online (from stores with a good return policy) so you can try it on in the comfort of your own room. Try everything on and ask, "What does this say about me?" You will quickly learn what makes you feel good and what feels off. Discard anything that makes you feel too junior, too mature, too trendy, or too sexy. You want a closet full of clothes that make you feel confident when you put them on.

Prove you're paying attention.

The details can make or break your whole look—and the way others perceive you. Have you ever heard the high-pitched clacking of a pair of heels that are so worn down that the metal is hitting the floor? How can you walk into any room with confidence when you're clicking down the hall? Perfectly great outfits and first impressions get ruined by a blouse that gaps across the bust, a skirt so short that your tush hits the chair, or pants so long that they bunch around your ankles. A good tailor is your best friend. You want people to focus on your ideas, not on weird outfit issues.

Upgrade your look to upgrade your role.

You know what kind of look is appropriate in your field, but you also want to stand out in the right way. Even if everyone is wearing jeans and sneakers to work, you want your jeans and sneakers to be elevated. Are the women in your business wearing pumps and pencil skirts? Make sure yours show a smidge of personal flair and an attention to detail. That's how you'll command attention in the right way. To look the part, you have to upgrade your hair too. You should not have the same haircut you had in college.

Never stop evolving.

You're not in high school; you shouldn't be shopping in the same stores you did back then. Keep looking for ways to elevate your style. A black blazer from Express is great at first. When you're ready to move up at work, you might move up to one from Theory. When you're ready for the Big Job, that blazer will be Stella McCartney. Take stock in your look every season and tweak it to match your place in the world.

presentations, running meetings, heading up projects—has put you one small step ahead on your journey. You didn't know how to run a meeting until you did it—you watched other people and learned, and then refined your technique until you could do it without thinking twice.

I'd known deep down for a long time that I could be the editor-in-chief of a magazine, but it took a few years to actually become that person. It wasn't until my third time at bat that I got the Big Job. The first time, I had the opportunity to pitch an entirely new magazine—my idea! I prepped at home for weeks with magazines spread all over the floor of my one-bedroom apartment. I had done demographic research, advertising-market overviews, competitive analyses . . . I'd never looked at my business this way in this much depth, but I was treading into new territory because it mattered that much to me. Most importantly, I had a vision for how this magazine would help the reader, as well as a stack of books and articles that backed up the need for this magazine to exist. My boss helped me get in front of her boss, Cathie Black, then-president of Hearst Magazines. I was so nervous and *very* rehearsed—I pulled out my reports and talking points. At one point, Cathie told me to put away my note cards and just *talk*. She actually let the idea incubate a bit—she liked it! I met other editors and execs to workshop the concept. But ultimately, it wasn't in the business plan for the company. Still, I learned a lot about how to create a brand and how to pitch an idea. And for the first time, my name popped out of a sea of other editors as someone who could possibly, maybe, one day be an editor-in-chief.

And then, a year and a half later, I got the call to pitch for the top job at a major magazine. This time, making the pitch wasn't as heavy a lift. I knew how to make a compelling proposal, as well as what *not* to do in my presentation (there were no note cards). I had a killer idea and a look to match: I bought a crazy-expensive Stella McCartney blazer and paired it with a cheap H&M tank—the perfect combo of aspirational and accessible, illustrating my vision for the magazine. No one needed to know that the tags were still on that blazer and if I didn't get the job, it was going back to the store. But in one weird moment, as I was on the way out the door for the pitch, I threw up in my bathroom. I'd never done that before. I hadn't even realized I was that nervous. But it was a sign that something was off. And it was: I never got to make my pitch. As I walked down the hall toward the meeting, I was pulled aside and told that someone else had already gotten the job. And it wasn't because my idea wasn't killer or I couldn't have done great things with that magazine. It wasn't my turn. The other editor was 10 years further along in her career, and this time, it was her shot.

A year passed before I had another opportunity, but by the time I was up for the job at *Seventeen,* I knew in my gut that I was ready. I owned my space and had no doubts about what I was going to say. For me, there would be no learning curve—I had the confidence to say so and the experience to back it all up. And, again, my outfit was killer: a Diane von Furstenberg fitted boiled-wool blazer, Gucci stilettos, and a razor-sharp pencil skirt—no tags needed; these were my clothes. (Tip: You know you're ready when the clothes for the job you want are already hanging in your closet.) Everything about my presentation said, *This woman is serious. This chick can do the job.*

In fact, in a postpitch email, Cathie Black asked me why I was the right person for the job and how badly I wanted it.

"There is no one who knows this generation of women

better than I do," I wrote back. "And no one knows how to create a magazine about the things that matter to them better than I do—because they matter to me too."

I felt it. It might have been a flash of ego, but no one has ever accused editors-in-chief of being shy.

It was true. And Cathie knew it. She offered me the job the next day. Every success (and mistake, actually), both big and small, had led me to that moment. I didn't know exactly where I was headed at every move along the way, but I trusted that everything I was doing would get me somewhere great.

EARN YOUR PLACE AT THE TABLE

Your calendar is probably full of meetings. But how often does it happen that no one even looks your way? You feel *disposable*. Kind of like one of those bottles of Poland Spring that everyone takes swigs out of but never finishes. When you are actually called on, it's not for your opinion; it's usually to take notes or to fetch something. And so, when you have an idea or a thought that would add to the conversation, you don't feel like it will be taken seriously, so you sit quietly. So painful.

That feeling of being invisible is what Sasha, 26, describes when I ask her the question I always ask at Badass Babe dinners: "If I could solve any problem, what would it be?" Sasha's eyes light up when she talks about her private-equity investing job. Despite the crazy-long hours and loads of pressure, there's also phenomenal opportunities for travel, meeting interesting people, and being part of some of the juiciest deals on Wall Street. And yet, she has a nagging sense that she's not taken seriously at work—and that she never will be. "I really want managers, executives, and investors to give me credit for the hard work I'm doing. I'll be sitting in a board-room, bringing up questions, but I just get overlooked," she says. "I look younger than my age; I'm petite; I'm Asian. Ninety-nine percent of the time, I'm in a room full of older men, I'm the only woman, the only minority. And when I ask questions, I get this look of *judgment*. It makes me not want to speak up. It's like I'm holding back and saving all the good questions for some shining moment, but rarely does that moment ever come."

This question comes up a lot, and it's always bothered me: How can I be taken seriously as a woman in a male-dominated industry? I have struggled with this for years, and the truth is, I don't have a good answer. I used to say that the key was to forget that you're a woman—you are a person with something important to say. Just say it. Don't go into a situation thinking that the deck is stacked against you or that your ideas won't be taken seriously; otherwise, that's the energy you'll project. But that's only half the battle. You might forget about being a woman or being a minority, but you have no control over how the men—typically white—on the other side of the table see you.

I want to focus on the part that you do have control over: being seen as too young to have a valid opinion. Sasha has been on the job for only 9 months; age aside, it's hard to give her opinion equal weight to that of a senior exec with a decade or more of experience. And yet, there are easy hacks around this.

Be prepared.

It's your obligation to use deep research to back up your ideas—that way, it's not just your opinion but unavoidable *facts*. Pre-sell your ideas to a few senior folks in quiet one-on-one meetings to get their feedback and get them on your side. Then, speak up at those meetings, present your ideas with authority, and ask those senior execs to back you up. A lot of times, your ideas won't land because all the person on the other side of the table will see is your 2 years of experience, but it's much harder to overlook well-researched, well-thought-through arguments.

Be indispensable.

How does a 24-year-old chick from rural New York find herself as the on-air producer for one of the biggest broadcast news anchors? Taylor, who had only some small-town TV experience before she landed a low-level gig at a major network, says she came in early, worked late, politely introduced herself to everyone on staff—from the major talent to the crew—and asked how she could be helpful. It seems so obvious, doesn't it? And yet volunteering to take on thankless, menial, entry-level tasks (that frankly have to get done by somebody), and then asking for more, will show people that you're capable, reliable, and confident. Once you've earned their trust, your point of view will carry real weight.

Don't stand for sneaky digs.

Sometimes, the challenge in being taken seriously doesn't come during a meeting but rather in the few minutes of chit-chat as everyone enters the room. Everyone's guard is down, and it's the little jokes and ribbing that can undermine you. Take Hannah, for example. At 26, she is leading an 11-person team and is the youngest manager her company has ever seen. But instead of inspiring admiration, she says, she feels like people think she got her job because she's the CEO's pet—or worse, his mistress! When a colleague made a snarky comment about her being the CEO's next wife, she called him out—in front of the whole room so her direct boss could hear. And he shut it down loud enough for everyone to hear that he had Hannah's back.

No matter how hard you're working at your job, you have to make it clear that you've earned your place at the table. Your only defense against misguided perceptions of you is to be prepared, indispensable, and strong. Be proud of seeing prejudices of *all kinds* and overcoming or working around them, or of sidestepping the small-minded people all together. A friend of mine says that with every prejudice she overcomes, she is more and more proud of her increased grit and resilience. She wears it as a badge of honor.

THE ENTITLEMENT SWIPE

Since we're discussing earning your place at the table, let's talk about the elephant in the room. You've seen the head-lines, and you know what older generations say about you: *entitled.*

Inevitably, when I tell senior executives that I'm writing a book about the power of millennial women, someone will pull me aside and say, "Ugh, what do you hate most about millennials?" And before I can set them straight (millennials are incredibly hardworking; demanding flexible schedules will change the working landscape for everyone!), they launch into a harangue about what *they* hate: how they find millennials lazy, entitled, and self-obsessed (as well as selfie-obsessed). You know the digs. Sure, it's easy to focus on the fact that you would probably rather call an Uber than take public transportation or hit up Task Rabbit instead of running a delivery across town. And even though you know you work really hard, when every lunch starts with an elaborately staged Instagram photo shoot, you can see how millennials have earned this rep.

Allie complains over a Badass Babes dinner that she feels "stalled." She works in retail operations at a big website that she's been dreaming of working for since she was in eighth grade. Allie has reached a point where she feels she knows more and is better qualified than her boss. "I've been getting frustrated a lot lately. I'm very confident in what I do. I know I'm good at my job, and I've worked really hard to get there. But I sort of feel like I'm taking a step back, and there's that frustration of feeling better, and I don't want to have that feeling. I don't want to be nasty about it, but it's that daily struggle." Allie is hungry for a promotion but feels stalled by all the rules. "I just had a really great review, but nothing has happened yet. Where do I even go from here? They say we have to wait, and I feel like that's kind of b.s. in a way. So many dates and deadlines and rules!" Allie's bosses don't see her frustration; they see that she's pushing hard against rules and systems that they're heavily invested in maintaining.

So listen: I have been that boss who wanted you to sit still and wait to get promoted. No matter how hard you were working, your project/taskforce/title change/raise wasn't in my strategic plan and probably wasn't in the budget. I've also been that young woman at the beginning of her career who had to dutifully file snoozy stories that were not my passion and go to every long, mind-numbing meeting in which nothing got done. I know that feeling in your soul that you have so much more to offer the world, if you could just get your shot. I saw my career as a straight line. Do a good job, get promoted; do a good job there, get promoted again. And that's how a lot of bosses think you should view your career too.

You're still new to the game, and like everyone else, you have to recognize that the world doesn't always do what you need when you need it to. While I am always 100 percent on your side, I can also see things from your bosses' side of the table. They see you walking into the room with 9 months' experience—which is everything to you—but from their perspective, it's just a blip on the screen. You see yourself as a carefully crafted brand, while your boss sees you as a tool to help get her job done. You've reached a part of your journey where you have a broad vision for yourself, and your boss is looking at you through only a small window. She's asking, "What can this person do for me, and how much is it worth to me?" She doesn't see where you're going or all the incredible strides you've made to get to this moment. Nor should she. You are slotted to fill a role inside your organization, and right now, the truth is that you're replaceable. The slot exists for a reason. It represents a job that needs to get done. It existed as a role for someone to fill before you, and it will be there after you move on to something bigger and better.

You see yourself as a carefully crafted brand, while your boss sees you as a tool to help get her job done.

It feels crappy, though, to think of yourself as a cog in the wheel, stripped of all your personality. That sense of yourself, and that incredibly big vision you had, may be similar to what your boss had for herself at your age. And then life happens— layoffs, cutbacks, breakups, difficult bosses. All this has shaped her life, and maybe she's feeling a little small about her own horizon. This isn't your concern or your problem to fix, but it's worth paying attention to.

You shouldn't have to manage your career based on someone else's ideas of how things should go, but ultimately, before you've earned your place at the table, you aren't in a position to make all the rules yet. Until it's time for you to take your seat, keep looking for chances to take twists and turns. Continue to push for more projects and let your boss know you think you're ready for greater responsibility (even if you're not going to get it right away). It's so much more interesting to be daring, to try new things, to be the young hotshot, and to risk being called "entitled" because you have been bold enough to go for something *big*.

ALL JOURNEY, NO DESTINATION

What if you could totally blow up the path to success and dictate the rules of your own journey? No out-of-touch bosses to make you feel clueless. No slow-and-steady climb waiting for promotions that never come or budgets to get approved. What if instead of twists and turns, you blazed an entirely new path? It's a pretty seductive idea, isn't it? One of the most interesting dinners I had was with a group of digital influencers—women with big Instagram, Twitter, or YouTube followings who have sponsors that pay to be included in a post. These women are the ultimate examples of chasing the newness—they have jobs that didn't even exist a few years ago. They are crusaders for respect in fields—fashion, beauty, cooking, and style—that have often been walled off from real power in the world and dismissed as "women's interest." They've created a new paradigm in which their tastes and experiences are prized, and they own their relationships with their fans and followers.

> "I'm a brand experiences director, which is a job that did not exist even 5 years ago. I'm really excited to find my next step in my career, and hopefully that is something that doesn't exist right now, so I can have some kind of hand in creating the future."
>
> **Delaney, 28**

> "I grew up in a very small town that has this dated idea of what life should be. You need to go to school, have a full-time job, and retire in the same place. I used to work in finance, and I started a blog for fun, putting together collages of clothes. One day, I was in a meeting and a hedge fund manager started complaining about his life.

I thought, 'I don't want to be complaining about my life. I don't think I can have a full-time job if it means being miserable.' I quit and started to build my blog into a business."

Carrie, 29

"I worked for an accessories company. I got sort of turned off by it. There was a lot of materialism, and I think it's important to look at the people who are higher up and be like, 'Do I want this life? Do they seem happy? Do they seem fulfilled?' At the time, the blog I'd been doing since college was gaining a following, and I decided to make the leap to doing it full-time. It doesn't feel like a job, and I've been able to support myself."

Brie, 25

YOUR TALENT IS GREATER THAN YOUR ABILITY TO PHOTOGRAPH AVOCADO TOAST

It's tantalizing to think that you can get paid for something you do anyway, like curating an amazing social media presence. But don't quit your day jobs just yet; the women who have done this successfully have seriously hustled. They described long hours spent strategizing how to reach sponsors, late nights of crafting images just so, and how they'd race to new brunch spots to get pics of pancakes or artfully arranged yogurt parfaits before other influencers get there.

One woman even started an Instagram for her dog so she'd have broader sponsorship opportunities.

What's not fun about that? But where is all this newness leading? These women list a few megastar influencers as their ultimate goal: Chiara Ferragni of the Blonde Salad, Emily Weiss of Into the Gloss, and Leandra Medine of Man Repeller. These women have built massive lifestyle businesses on the backs of posts about outfits and shots of celeb-y friends. They are the supermodels of the influencer world.

But just like every pretty girl can't be the next Gigi Hadid, every blogger can't be the new Man Repeller. The flip side of working with all that newness is often an anxiety about what comes next, after the shininess has worn off.

> "I feel like tomorrow, you just never know. I worry about staying relevant with all the new social media changes coming up. Like, will my following transfer?"
>
> **Brie, 25**

> "I don't have an exact image of where I want to be in the next 10 to 15 years, but I know that it's an ambitious one, and it's something incredible or high up, and I don't know how to get there. And that's the anxiety—having the vision of myself as an influencer and not knowing what's next."
>
> **Blair, 22**

"It's kind of scary, because what I do is so singular right now. What am I going to do when that's not the next big thing? There's a lot of anxiety that goes into thinking what's next for yourself."

Kate, 24

"Right now, it's hard to visualize. In my mind, I know what I want to do. I know what my end goal is. I work toward that, and I'll accept whatever change comes."

Carrie, 29

ARE YOU ALL DESTINATION AND NO JOURNEY?

I met a woman who revealed that she'd so singularly pursued one job at one particular company that she was totally lost when she didn't get it. I suggested another company in the same industry. She wasn't interested. I suggested a similar job in an adjacent industry. Nope—no go. I suggested other ways to use her skills that might give her a comparable feeling of satisfaction. She didn't want to hear it. She was all in—but in the wrong way. We all have that idea about the Dream Job, but the importance of the dream is chasing it. What does the Dream Job represent to you: Adventure? Respect? Meaning? Creative fulfillment? These feelings are your real destination.

THE CAREER THAT'S ALL YOU

There's something powerful about having the courage to be all you when building your career. To create these opportunities, pay attention to what feels good and find new places to make a mark where nobody has before. Frankly, it's a lesson for all of us to find a place in the world where we can be our authentic selves. But how do you grow? The answer is not getting the brunch intel faster or finding new ways to stage an OOTD. You're building a brand, learning how to market a product, developing audience-development protocols, mastering talent management, and figuring out contract negotiation. And so then comes the question that *every* Badass Babe in every field has to answer at some point: What is your unique perspective on the world, and how can you convince people to see things your way? Don't let anybody try to fence you in with old ideas of how work should work. Yours is not a journey with no destination. For you, the journey *is* the destination.

EXPECT BUMPS ALONG THE WAY

Every chick who is living the Big Life encounters a "what's next?" moment along the way.

I've had to face sharp turns too. After 7 happy and amazing years, my job as the editor-in-chief of *Seventeen* ended. In the face of a disastrous economic downturn for print magazines, the brand was reorganized and half the staff was let go. I was honored to do that job for as long as I did, and I'm nothing but proud of the work my team did there. That outcome wasn't exactly how I would have scripted it, but that's how life works. There's no avoiding all the bumps and bruises unless you're so ultra-careful that you only make safe choices. And where's the badassery in that?

Getting everything out of your Big Life means getting comfortable with being uncomfortable. An epic journey is never clean and pretty. There are dark moments—quests are full of confusion and surprises, and sometimes it's impossible to imagine how you're going to come out on the other side. But you grow stronger along the way too; you get to know yourself better—and you gain clarity about what matters most. You'll soon see you're not so easily derailed by a snipe from an annoying boss. That chick who got promoted so quickly? You don't have a second to be jealous, and you *know* your turn is coming. The cutie you just started seeing after countless Tinder dates gone wrong? He's there for you after you've spent yet another long night finishing up a big project you conceived at work, and he's made dinner. Sure, you're still chasing the newness, and that means there are more challenges, *harder* ones even. Truth is, you're never really going to have a moment where you think, "I've arrived. This is it."

But if your journey has taught you anything so far, it's that you'll tackle whatever life throws at you like the true badass you are.

THE BIG LIFE
CONVERSATION

ALICIA MENENDEZ
Anchor of Fusion

HOW SHE EARNED HER PLACE AT THE TABLE— AND WHY SHE WANTS YOU TO SIT NEXT TO HER!

When I first saw Alicia Menendez, anchor of Fusion news, she was hosting a panel to help a group of very senior media execs understand millennials. She was the youngest woman in the room by 20 years! She had such a fun, funny attitude and a no-b.s. POV—which has become her on-air trademark—that her opening remarks stuck with me: "I am a millennial now, and I will be a millennial in 5 years and in 10 years. I will always be a millennial." Her point to the assembled crowd was that the changes that are happening for this generation—*because* of this generation—are going to change the world. And while you might look at your assistant and wonder what she's thinking now, someday she's going to be the boss, so show her some respect!

Ann: When you were 16, growing up in Union City, New Jersey, how did you imagine your life would be now?

Alicia: I grew up in a really feminist household, where both my parents worked full-time out of the home. My parents were public servants, so I always assumed that I would go to law school directly after college, as my father had done, practice law for a few years, and then run for office and also be a public servant. I also was really aware of the possibility that that might not leave room for a husband or children. That is something that I grappled with at a really young age. I felt that I wanted to do what I wanted to do, and if that meant there were going to be personal sacrifices, then so be it.

AS: So how did you get from that dream to being the anchor of a game-changing news network?

AM: After I graduated college, I worked on some political campaigns and realized how much power the media had. I had never really thought about media beyond my consumption of it. And all of a sudden, it was like all these worlds opened up. I had taken the LSAT, I had my letters of recommendation done, and my applications were ready to go, but I realized I didn't actually want to go to law school. And while I would love to be a public servant, I didn't know why I needed to do that right then. It was like all of a sudden, all these possibilities opened up. All those professional responsibilities became all these personal possibilities of not defining my life—and not constricting it—as I had always imagined.

AS: Much of your reporting is through the lens of diversity— particularly aimed at millennials in America who are the most diverse generation ever. Does your identity as Latina or a second-generation American change the way you think about success?

AM: I definitely think being second-generation changes things. I still feel an immense responsibility to give back. I grew up upper-middle class with two college-educated, English-speaking,

US-citizen parents in a town where most people didn't have any of those things. I started out with so much privilege relative to my peers that I always felt I had to do *something* with that gift. And then, because I was living and learning in such close proximity to people who had less, I learned very quickly that I wasn't necessarily smarter or better—I'd simply had advantages that other people didn't have. And that comes with a responsibility to get in rooms that people aren't, to sit at tables that people aren't at, so that other people can say, "Wow, Alicia is really great. We need more people like Alicia in this room; we need more people like Alicia at this table." And when someone is talking about *me*, normally what that means is we need more *young people*, we need more *women*, we need more *Latinas*. And so there's the sense that every time I do something, every time I talk about something, I'm not really just talking for myself. And there's a lot riding on my success or my failure.

AS: That's a lot of personal pressure.

AM: Listen, there's plenty of therapy and coaching in dealing with all of this! [*laughs*]

AS: How are you personally helping other young women or Latinas get a seat at the table?

AM: If anyone reaches out to me—I happen to get women, people of color, and young people—and they want to know how to break into television, I feel like it's my responsibility to get on the phone with them or look at their tapes and actually give back in that way. Because when I was coming up through this industry—and I still feel like I'm coming up—I just did not feel like there were a lot of people who I could turn to and ask for that kind of help. And it's hard. Whether it's television or investment banking, you're navigating a system blindly, and that is a lot harder than navigating it with the help of someone who has already done it.

I did not start in my Dream Job. I started doing 6:00 a.m. Saturday-morning spots where I would be followed by a dog who swallowed a diamond. And then making the jump to actually being a host and getting paid—that took me 3 years probably. And the entire time, the way I did it, I held down a full-time paid job and worked at nonprofits and think tanks while I pursued television.

AS: Do you still have side hustles that you're working on?

AM: Oh my gosh, yes. Yes. I have a book proposal that I am working on. I have a scripted series that I'm working on. There should always be more options. I have a lot of ideas. I consume a lot of media, and I'm really critical about what I think is missing. I feel like you can either wait for other people to create the thing you want, or you can create it for yourself. It's not like I wake up in the morning and I'm like, "I'm amazing and I ought to share all these gifts with the world." Every time I approach one of these projects, I'm like, "Who the hell am I? Why am I the one to do this? This is ridiculous; I should just go back to bed." And the challenge is being like, "No, I have an idea and I need to be involved in the doing of it." Everyone wants to be a writer. Everyone wants to be on television. Well, then you actually have to do the writing. You actually have to tell the story. And so as long as I focus on the doing, then it helps me get over myself.

AS: So despite your early ideas that there wasn't room in your life for ambition and a partner, you got married recently!

AM: Yes! I made all my ambitions really clear up-front, and Carlos got it from the get-go. I wanted him to know what he was getting into. And I wasn't really scared of scaring him off, because if I had scared him off, then he wasn't the right person. So, I ended up with someone who was equally ambitious, equally intense, and equally mindful of this idea of giving back. And I just don't think I would be happy married to any other type of person.

How did you know that Carlos was the right partner for you?

AM: When we met, I worked at a nonprofit and was pursuing television on the side. He worked at the White House. We met in DC, and about 2 years into dating, I got offered a job in New York at the *Huffington Post*, and he got offered a job in Florida. We each got offered a Dream Job in tandem, and we had to come to an agreement as a couple to each take the job we wanted and to stay together. And he was very willing to move to New York and be with me, because he understood the opportunity I was being offered was very rare and that it was the step I needed to take in order to pursue what we'd been talking about since the day we'd met.

Together, we decided that he should take the job in Miami, I'd take the job in New York, and our relationship was strong enough for us to live apart for a while. A year later, I got my job at Fusion in Miami. But that test taught me that, (a) he was willing to make sacrifices, and (b) we were both willing to come to the table, really consider what was in our own and in each other's best interests, and be able to evaluate that as a couple. It affirmed for me that he was the person I wanted to marry. Life will throw things like that at us a million more times, and the fact that we were battle-tested before we made a legal commitment to one another was a big deal.

8

STOP WITH THE WHAT-IFS

FIND A PARTNER
WHO HONORS YOUR AMBITION
AND STOP WORRYING ABOUT
BABIES FOR NOW

It's 3:00 a.m. and you bolt awake with one crystal-clear thought: You will be alone forever. You shake it off and force yourself back to sleep. It's stress, you think. Or maybe that third margarita. Of course you're worthy of love, you tell yourself. You just have to try harder, meet more people, make more time for friends where social possibilities start to open up. And yet, every evening that you settle into your couch with the dating apps open on your phone, you feel further and further away from that love you know you deserve. The people you swipe past seem interchangeable, disposable even. The semi-sleazy come-ons are predictable by now. You've had the hookups. You've been on every coffee date/walk-and-talk/meditation meetup/happy hour/midnight rendezvous. Every once in a while, there's a spark—a bit of sizzle with someone sexy who leans in and kisses your neck in a way that reminds you about the closeness you're missing. And yet the heat always cools. Travel, work, family, schedules . . . something always gets in the way. You're not even looking for commitment—you just want *connection*. And the harder you go after it, the quicker it seems to slip away.

And so you double down on work. Sound familiar? You tell yourself that this is your chance to focus on getting ahead. Block out the distractions of dating. Stay away from any emotional drama that steals energy from your real passion right now: career. And yet, that 3:00 a.m. wakeup call keeps coming. Why haven't you met anyone? It must be your fault. You're too picky. Too demanding. Too busy. And then you have this sad resigning thought: What if I *never* meet someone?

I've heard versions of this story again and again. "I've worked my ass off for the last 7½ years. I know what I want to do with my career. I've created my own position. My company is paying me everything I want," says Tiffani, 33. "Now, when am I going to meet the right person? When is that part of my life going to fall into place?"

For Olivia, 26, finding someone steady has started to feel like a competition. She could be killing it in every other part of her life, but the women who had found a partner were one-up on her. "One month this person is engaged, the next *this* person is engaged. The next month, this person is pregnant, and your whole life is baby showers and wedding showers. This is terrible," she explains. "The older I get, the more I start to feel lonely."

For Marley, 28, the grind of nonstop dating since college has worn her down. "You would think that in New York, arguably the center of ambition in the United States, it would be easy to find a guy who knows what he wants. But most guys don't," she says. "My job and my ambition have become an issue with any guy I've dated since I was 19. They're like, I'm uncomfortable because you know what you want and I don't. So in the beginning, these guys truly think in their heart of hearts they want an ambitious girl, a passionate person. And then they have to examine their own passion, and they realize they don't have it and you do, and *that* makes them uncomfortable."

Fresh from a difficult breakup, Piper, 26, has sworn off dating and wants to fast-forward to the snuggling-on-the-couch part. "This whole single shit is killing me. I'm just not interested," she says. "I just want a wife and a dog. I want companionship, partnership, a *ride or die*."

If this sounds like the same old *Sex and the City* when-will-I-find-love anxiety, it's not. You want more out of life and out of your relationship than just being loved. Sure, you want to date someone who is attractive, hardworking, smart, funny . . . check, check, check, check. But you also want a person who shares your dreams, respects your goals, and wants to help you reach them. Your partner will be your ultimate teammate—committed to being by your side as you figure out the next phase of your Big Life *together*. And you want your team to win.

My job here isn't to find you that ideal partner and deliver him or her wrapped up in a bow—the last thing you want is more pat advice about how and where to meet someone. This chapter isn't about solving all of your dating problems either. It's about putting all this anxiety into perspective.

I, too, have felt that 3:00 a.m. panic. I have never told this story publicly before, but I was 34 and single when I was up for the editor-in-chief position at *Seventeen*. I'd had a relationship through most of my 20s, and I'd been having fun dating in my early 30s. I was finally making good money—as did most of the guys I went out with—so dinners, fancy cocktails, and fun getaways were now part of the picture. While it was great most of the time, I knew that ultimately I wanted to find a partner . . . and no one seemed to fit. And just as the opportunity to pitch for the Big Job came up, I panicked. What if I didn't have time to date? Shouldn't I spend less time at work and more time trying to meet a man? I seriously considered not throwing my hat in the ring for the job. Surprisingly a lot of people around me sort of nodded and agreed when I told them my fears. Yes, they agreed, successful women are intimidating to most men. Yes, you will be too busy to go to all the parties and all the dinners where you might meet someone.

But it was my closest girlfriend who said the one thing that mattered most: "Well, dating isn't working out so well for you right now. You may as well focus on your career and see what happens."

She was right. It wasn't until I had the Big Job that I really felt ready to share my life with someone. I needed my own domain for my sense of personal success. I needed to see what I was capable of achieving on my own before I started to make life decisions with someone else. And it's true, a lot of guys I'd been dating were intimidated by my position at first. (Hell, I was probably intimidated by my position at first.) But the one who wasn't was the one I wanted to be with. Turns out, the Big Job made me a more self-assured and more interesting person, and it was then that I was able to connect with a self-assured, fascinating guy who had his own ambitions but thought mine were pretty amazing too.

I'm not saying my path to finding a partner and starting a family is the one you should take. I was 35 when I met Richard at a random bar on a girls' night out. We had an instant connection. I was 39 when we got married, 40 when my son was born, and almost 42 when my daughter arrived. That's a long time to wait—emotionally and biologically. But I tell you my story now to show you the *possibilities*. Maybe you'll get married and have children before you turn 30. Maybe you'll decide to have children on your own at 38. Maybe you'll swear off all dating until you've made executive vice-president. Maybe you'll freeze your eggs. Maybe your high-school crush was the right one for you after all. Maybe you'll have a series of emotionally involved relationships with people you travel to see a couple of times a year, or maybe you'll scrap them all in one swoop for a partner who is waiting at home with a glass of wine at the end of a long day.

You need to see this piece of your Big Life as an opportunity to craft a relationship exactly the way you want it, instead of a rapidly dwindling chance to lock it in before you turn 30/run out of eggs/all the good ones get married . . . or whatever scary scenarios are running around in your head.

It seems obvious, but it can be overlooked in the franticness of dating: It matters very much who you allow in your life—whether it's your boyfriend, your girlfriend, your husband, your partner, your wife. It's important that the people you surround yourself with set you up for success in all areas of your life.

You are not beholden to anyone else's ideas of how a relationship should go. You owe it to yourself to figure out what you need in a partner—with the same ambition and rule-bending attitude that you bring to shaping your career. And once you do, the stronger and more confident you can be in your quest, and the more likely you are to get what you need.

WORKING FOR THE RELATIONSHIP IS PART OF YOUR JOB

Hannah is on the way up in her career. A giant corporation brought her into the fold to disrupt its sleepy services. At 26, she oversees a team of 11 people, has launched a whole new product for the company, and knows that she's being eyed for bigger and better roles. Every night, with the same intensity that she brings to her day job, she goes home and goes through each of the apps on her phone: Tinder, Hinge, Happn, Bumble. "I have like 900 apps! It's a chore," she says. "I get home at night, and I'm like, I need to go through them! It's 11:00 p.m., and I'm like, crap! I forgot to do my swipes." At work, Hannah can see the straight line between her hard work and professional reward. But in her personal life, putting in so much effort and seeing no return makes her feel like a dud. "I am sure I date more than any human imaginable," she says. "There was a period of time when I was going on four dates a week. I'd meet someone for a drink at 7:00, have dinner with a friend at 8:00—*never* eat on a first date—and then book a date for a drink after dinner."

Her approach might be a little over the top, but when it comes to first dates, Hannah has a clear-cut way to judge whether the guy is getting a second: "I go on the first date. If I can't marry you, I never see you again—it's clearly working," she says with a laugh, although she's not really kidding.

She puts on a happy-ish face about her single life, as if it's a bit madcap to date with such fervor, but it still stings that she's solo for most major life events. She's the youngest of three sisters and measures her personal success against theirs. "At my sister's bridal shower," Hanna tells me, "a relative came over and said, 'It's a big year for your family: One sister is getting married, another sister is having a baby.' And then there was this awkward pause and she goes, 'You have your career.'" Ugh.

It's exhausting to work so hard at something and come up empty at every turn. You've been there. You're booking tons of coffee dates only to be let down when the guy talks non-stop about urban cycling and doesn't ask a thing about you. The occasional hookup gives you a sexy boost, but it's a bummer that you don't want to follow up a night of hot sex with a leisurely brunch the next morning. And it doesn't help when every day, some college friend posts pics of an elegant but rustic wedding held in a picture-perfect barn. And damn it! It was your idea to have food trucks at your wedding!

Hard work isn't new to you. You're dealing with tough salary negotiations, senior team members who don't get you, challenging projects, and backstabbing coworkers. You're putting in the work, every day, because you want to have a kick-ass career that you're superpassionate about. You know that your career is something that takes supreme effort, but there's no question in your mind that you'll eventually get where you want to be. You understand that while you'd love to land that ultimate job tomorrow, it's likely to take time—there are still lessons to be learned and moves to be made. Deep in your soul, you understand that the Big Job isn't something you can magically pull out of the air and effortlessly enjoy forever after. The Big Job is hard stuff, and you're willing to do the work.

So, why is it so difficult for you to channel that same level of understanding—and patience—when it comes to dating?

It's admittedly easier to brush off work obstacles, since they are part of the challenge of building your career. We've all faced letdowns on the job—it stings when you don't get the go-ahead for a big project or a client doesn't jump on board with an idea you're crazy excited about. Sure, sometimes there's a brief moment where you internalize it as a personal failure, but ultimately, you know that you can't control everything that happens at work, and you move on. If only it were so easy to brush off disappointments in the relationship department. When someone you're seriously interested in ghosts after date three, or a relationship you have high hopes for doesn't work out, it just plain hurts. Let it hurt—*for a while*. But remind yourself that love, like work, isn't completely under your control. No matter how amazing, smart, sexy, funny, and beautiful you are, there's going to be someone who doesn't get on board . . . *and that's not your fault.*

Some Badass Babes who are working hard in the dating department have managed to channel that feeling of not knowing into *anticipation.* They're doing the work, but they're also allowing themselves to get excited about the rewards they know will eventually come.

Sydney, who has worked hard to embrace the mess of her life—transitioning from a high-paying sales job to the wild world of being an entrepreneur—found that she had to purposefully prioritize finding a relationship. "I put my man and a ring on my vision board . . . as well as the word *orgasm!*" Sydney says. "It hasn't happened yet. Well, the orgasms have, but I have a great vibrator."

For Jordan, her personal life got unstuck at the same time her professional life did. She'd been agonizing about an intractable management problem at her nonprofit for what had felt like ages when, suddenly, a brighter opportunity landed in her lap. While she had been doing the work, when the guy came, it too felt like he had arrived out of nowhere.

"I went on two OkCupid dates. One at 5:00 p.m. and one at 7:45 the same night," Jordan says. "The 5:00 p.m. was so terrible I almost canceled the 7:45, but I didn't. And it was *him.* We've been serious since about 10 minutes into that date. We're traveling together, and he's going to meet my family later this summer."

In your career, you aren't letting anyone else determine your future. You're taking control, making moves, and enjoying the ride as you see your hard work start to take you places. Crafting the right relationship takes the same amount of dedication, careful negotiation, and faith that you will get where you want to be. And just as every bad boss or less-than-stellar performance review is part of a process that will eventually bring you to the happy career place you want to be in, every bad date gets you a notch closer to being ready for the Big Love you know you deserve.

DON'T GET STUCK ON HOW THINGS "SHOULD BE"

When Grace was growing up, she didn't have any trouble envisioning her Big Life. Her life to-do list included everything from European travel and working for the UN to landing a major six-figure job soon after graduation. She's earned the confidence that if there's something she wants, she can get it. Grace speaks passionately about her job, her squad, and the biz she's incubating on the side—it's clear that she has a big vision for these areas of her life. There's a different tone, though, when she talks about her boyfriend. "The couple that holds hands and skips across the street? That's not us," she says. "I call him when I'm stressed. He listens to me vent, but that doesn't really count as being *supportive*."

Grace has been with her guy for years, but she still feels reservations about whether he's the right partner for her. Her boyfriend is a highly educated African-American man who also worked his way out of a lower-income neighborhood, like she did, and who also has huge ambitions for his career and family. He wants to get married. Grace, who has just crossed that 30-year-old mark, says she does too. But she's not ready yet. She's looking for a sign that he's the right man for her.

On paper, her boyfriend is perfect. Together, they're a power couple. He makes her work harder, strive toward more. But just as Grace hadn't felt sure about what really makes her happy in a job, she's not sure what makes her happy in a relationship either. This is the guy she *should* be with, but is he the one she *wants* to be with?

She's not sure—and that drives her nuts. "My parents have been married for 43 years. My mom saw my dad out of a window and they just *knew*," she explains.

Why can't she be as sure about marriage as her parents were? That's her 3:00 a.m. panic.

Grace is stuck on a fantasy story of how relationships should play out: Find someone who matches your ambition, someone with the same background, similar dreams, and you'll just *know*. It's this idea about what love should be like that I've heard echoed again and again around my dinner table.

It's a pretty seductive feeling for an ambitious girl to be with a partner who sees so much potential in her that he or she sets the bar even higher and makes her strive even harder. But what if you've set the bar just high enough for yourself? What if an ambitious girl really needs a partner who will help diffuse the stress of her day or celebrate the small wins instead of asking what it's all laddering up to? Just asking yourself the question makes all the difference, no matter what the answer is for you.

When I first started the interviews for this book, I'd expected the most ambitious women to want to be with partners who could match their intensity. But that hasn't always been the case. Rosie, a chef with goals of making herself a name-brand, gushes when she talks about her relationship with a police officer. She's not looking for a Mr. Big; she's not aiming to be one-half of a power couple. She's interested in being in love and being happy. "When we met, I told him I worked really crazy hours and that I'm very dedicated to my job, and my career comes first," she says. "He was never intimidated by that, and that's one of the things I liked about him right away."

(continued on page 174)

BADASS DUDES DINNERS: WHY IS IT SO HARD TO MAKE A CONNECTION?

I have spent my career understanding the inner workings of women, but men, in so many ways, are still a mystery to me. And so, armed with the dating questions that are on heavy rotation in young women's minds, I set up a small series of dinners with dudes. This was not exhaustive research (next book—promise!), but these guys got honest over pizza and wine about some of the weirdness they feel about dating, relationships, and love. (Except for the one 23-year-old guy who couldn't be honest about anything! He lied about his age, texted all through dinner, guzzled wine, and bragged about sleeping with three women at a time while tricking them into thinking they were the only one in his bed. This guy doesn't deserve to date any Badass Babe ever. Avoid! Avoid! Avoid!)

"I feel like she's *too* into me."

George, 30, runs his own tech company, meditates regularly, and says he's also great at cooking breakfast. "My problem is that the women I go out with put me on a pedestal. They think I'm perfect."

Ben, 28, a graphic designer/indie rocker adds, "I'll go out with a woman, and she's into me so fast. It's like she wants to go wherever I want to go."

Hold up. These guys are great, but I find it hard to

believe that smart, confident women are falling all over themselves to follow them around with no feedback that their devotion is returned. And then Ben's friend Olivia, who's brought him to my dinner, says the thing that puts it all into perspective: "When I was younger and first met a guy, I would generally do what he wanted to do. It wasn't necessarily because I was super into him," she explains. "I didn't have the confidence to say what I wanted to do or to ask him to come to my thing."

It's one of those eye-opening moments that makes you go back through your last seven dates to see if you've also fallen into this trap. You think you're being accommodating. He thinks you're fawning over him! This is not a call to bring back *The Rules*, in which you had to pretend to be too busy for dates to hook a guy. The. Worst. But it's a reminder that the things you're interested in doing are the things that make you *interesting*!

"Talking about her job feels like a test."

The question I hear over and over from young women is, "How do I find a man who isn't intimidated by my ambition?" But I also hear from men that they want a partner who is smart, focused, *and* ambitious. So, why does it seem like dudes are so easily turned off by your big dreams?

"When you first meet a woman, and she's talking about the ins and outs of her job, sometimes it feels like she's making a guy jump through hoops—like talking about her job is a test," explains Trevor, a badass finance guy who is married to an equally Badass Babe working her Dream Job in the tech industry. "It's entirely possible that if a woman thinks a guy is zoning out when she's talking about her job, it's not because he's turned off by her ambition, but because he's thinking, 'She's talking about her job and I don't know a thing about her yet.'"

I can see that. When work is the center of your focus for 18 hours a day, it can be hard to turn down the volume on that part of your brain as soon as you leave the office. Even when you're out with friends, you're still figuring out the weird dynamics of the office, mentally practicing for your next presentation, or obsessing over the details of the project that's waiting on your desk. And so, while you're talking about the things that are top-of-mind for you, he wants to unwind from a long day too, and would rather hear about your last vacay or the art exhibit you're dying to see. He probably wants to share a bit about his own ambitions too. You can't turn the dial up to 11 all the time. You have to learn to craft your message and your timing in order to make a real connection. Obviously, your career is a big part of who you are and it's important, but let him get to know you as a person before the convo is filled up by the latest office drama.

"It's not a numbers game."

There's this awful, self-defeating idea out there that you have to date a lot to find someone who is right for you. That's the mind-set that makes you schedule five Tinder dates a week, sends you to dollar-beer nights to suffer through dimwitted conversation with a no-fee-rental broker, and tells you that you should go out with the random guy scoping you out at Walgreens. And yet, I haven't heard from any of the guys that they feel the same urgency to churn numbers to meet The One.

Once you stop putting up a façade about who you think the other person wants you to be, you can connect on a more authentic level, says Ben, the graphic designer. And Derek, 27, who works for a nonprofit, takes it one step further: "Be purposeful and have an idea of what you want," he says. "Not necessarily a checklist, because life doesn't go according to plan. But a general idea of what you're looking for. Be intentional in dating."

Not that you need anyone's permission to name what you want to claim, but it's nice to hear that dudes are on the same page, isn't it?

173

Allison, who is dealing with the stress of running her own tech start-up that teaches women how to code, admits she's the "alpha married to the beta." But she's eased into a place where she enjoys being the breadwinner. "We met on a photo shoot. I just like him. He's kind and warm, and I'm 100-percent okay being the primary breadwinner." Would she rather be with a guy who's as driven as she is? "It doesn't feel like the kind of thing where you can say this is what I want and get it," Allison says. "Do I want a pony and a million dollars? Sure, but . . . I like *him*."

It's an important reminder that love doesn't always look the way you expect it to. And when you meet someone who sparks your imagination, a new vision of a life together revolves around the ways you complement each other.

Take Tasha, for example. "I met my husband right out of college. He's 15 years older than I am. I was working in marketing at my first job, and he was my client who was looking for his second act," she explains. In rapid succession, they got married and launched a new business together. But Tasha wanted something more for herself, and so she went back to school to get a degree in nursing. Then she got pregnant, and all her plans changed. Now, at 27, she's strategizing around school and a baby and hoping that her husband can sell the business in a year so he can be home at night when she's pulling 12-hour shifts to get her degree. "This is not how I saw my life playing out," Tasha says. "He's the best thing that's ever happened to me. But I want to know that I'll get to finish what I started, that I'll get to pursue what I want to pursue."

Tasha had to reimagine how her desire for her own domain fit in with a strong partner who had already achieved tremendous success in his life. But she's making it work.

Taylor, who is trying to squeeze in dating around her grueling schedule as a TV producer, is keeping as many options open as possible. Love, she says, doesn't have to follow anyone else's rules: "I don't like to have a label because I feel like that closes me off to any human being that might make me the happiest person in the world. That could be a girl, that could be a guy, that could be a guy that identifies as a girl . . . like, I really don't care, as long as that person is happy with who they are, and I'm happy with that person."

When you free yourself from the question of how things *should* be, or why your relationship isn't like your parents', those of the people around you, or the glamorous celeb couples who seem totally relaxed and uncomplicated, you can craft the relationship that works for *you*.

A RELATIONSHIP WON'T MAKE YOUR AMBITION DISAPPEAR

Jenny likes surprising people. She graduated college in 3 years to prove that she could. She left a fancy New York City job for a start-up stationed in the desert. We've talked a lot about how she can deepen and broaden her career, and I've given her a lot of counsel and a few key contacts over the years. Then, one day over coffee, she surprised me with this statement: "I am afraid that I'll have to dial back my ambition to have love, marriage, and a family." At the time, there was no boyfriend in the picture. She wasn't even dating. She wasn't even really looking. And yet, there was this abstract anxiety that somewhere out there was a partner and children that would make it impossible for her to live her dreams.

ROCK-STAR MOMS DINNER: HOW THEY BALANCE BIG CAREERS AND BIG FAMILY AMBITIONS

It's a small miracle when so many young women with demanding careers *and* demanding toddlers all make it to my place for pizza and wine one night. I was sure they were going to cancel at the last minute, claiming late deadlines, last-minute baby-related emergencies, husbands who have to stay at work and couldn't relieve the nannies, or babysitters who were too busy. I'd understand any excuse—their lives are complicated! But, they all managed to deal with work, husbands, and nannies, so they're free to talk about how they navigate their families and their careers.

"I don't make a ton of money, so I basically just pay for my child care. I love what I do, but it's not a huge financial contribution for our family," says Jean, a public defender. "But at the end of the day, I want to know that my kids will understand why I work so

hard and that they'll be happy about it. Or, are they going to ask why mom left all the time?"

"I had to de-scale my life to have children. I was working a ton, getting promoted, doing really well. But I was having breakfast, lunch, and dinner at the office. I would go into work on Saturdays—I would actually take naps on the floor of the office on the weekend," says Kelly, a certified financial planner. "My husband and I decided that I would take a step back when we got pregnant. But then I had an opportunity to continue working in a more sane way. I enjoy making money. I enjoy what I do. It's engaging, and I like the people I work with and the satisfaction I get every day."

"The way I make it work is just to be present in the moment. It's okay to be ambitious. It's okay to be a mom. Someday, I'm going to be so out of balance and have to put a lot of time into work—and that's okay," says Maureen, a pharmaceutical rep. "The thing that helped me realize it's okay to want to advance my career and be a mom was *acceptance*."

"Everybody sitting at the table is like, I love what I do," Kelly adds. "No one said, 'I hate my job and I wish I didn't have to go back to work after maternity leave.' Having passion for your career is what matters and makes you want to figure out how to make work and motherhood coexist. It doesn't matter how senior you are in your career. It's how passionate you are that changes everything."

She'd always imagined that she'd get married young, and she wants to have a lot of children, she says. But why does she think she can't have a big career, a big relationship, and a big family? I ask. After a long pause, she says that it's hard for her to put a finger on why. Her mom didn't work outside the home. Her friends planned to dial down their work when they started getting serious in love. But then came the important reveal: Her dreams are so big, she says, that it feels like there can be no room for a partner or a family *and* her ambition. It seems too hard.

The truth is, Jenny isn't afraid that she'll never find a guy who honors her ambition; she's afraid of her ambition itself. It feels so big that it takes up all the energy she might devote to falling in love.

Still, it's no fun to wonder if the cute guy sitting across from you is ready to help you manage career and children before you've even covered basic topics like where you grew up or what you studied in college. I've been asked these questions many times: "How will I manage a career and children? Will I have to give up my ambitions to be a parent? My mother stayed home with me, so shouldn't I do that too?"

Having a child is serious business, but there is no reason you should be worrying about nannies and school pick-up schedules at this stage of your Big Life.

The idea that you should have this all nailed down before you've removed your Tinder profile is an anxiety-producing toxic side-effect from the seemingly never-ending work-life balance conversation. But the reality is, right now, you don't even have the career to lean into or the family to balance! You're still building those parts of your Big Life! There are endless ways that family and relationships can work, and it all depends on what you and your partner decide works for you. There is no way you can predict what your situation will be and plan accordingly before the job/partner/baby have become an actual possibility. And yet, you can diffuse the anxiety you feel now by focusing on all the amazing ways you can craft the life you want. You're already doing it at your job by pushing for more freedom from the office, flexible hours, and equal pay. Apply the same kind of rule-bending thinking to building a relationship and a family.

NOT KNOWING IS THE HARDEST PART

Dating is equal parts exhilarating and exhausting. It's sexy fun to imagine yourself partnered with some of your hotter Tinder matches, even if the spark doesn't take off.

But sometimes, you just want to settle in with someone and order Thai food while watching TV—and wouldn't it be nice if you could have that person lined up by Friday? You want to be done swiping left or right *for good*. But you have a lifetime ahead of you to share take-out, TV nights in, sleeping late, sex, shopping, cooking, parties, holidays, vacations, and whatever else you envision in your relationship.

Sharing take-out on the sofa in your jammies with someone you love is wonderful, but less so if you've settled for a guy who isn't a real match for you. And while not knowing is hard, so are relationships—in the best way possible. So, forget about all the what-ifs that are undermining your sense of awesomeness. In this moment, focus on you—what you want and need. Let yourself grow into the most badass version of who you can be. That amazing version of you—confident, secure, interesting, and open—will attract an equally amazing partner. And you can start living the Big Life together.

9

THE PRESSURE TO BE PERFECT

THE DARK SIDE OF AMBITION

S cary feelings fester in dark corners.

When a hard-charging chick feels like her life is out of control, and she can't fix the bigger problems, it's easy to start fixating on the little things—the ones you can control.

And yet, if you've ever rubbed a stain too hard or pulled the loose thread of a sweater, you know that sometimes, the harder you try to fix the problem, the worse it gets, and the faster everything unravels.

Jenny is as wholesome and sweet as the small Midwestern town she hails from. Her tireless work ethic and bubbly personality helped her land the Dream Job at her favorite magazine right away. "I thought I would have this instantly glamorous life. Which totally wasn't true," she says. "I moved to New York City with no friends, no money, and no real housing—I had a temporary sublet that was awful."

Jenny realized how lucky she was to have landed a coveted gig, but for a first job, things were intense. Her boss was crazy busy and expected her to show up knowing the ropes. There was no time for a learning curve. Jenny also expected the same from herself, which was even worse. It was hard for her to accept that she had so much to learn, or that something seemingly as simple as coordinating a calendar or doing background research for a presentation was beyond her skills.

Jenny struggled to get her bearings, and that's when an eating disorder that she thought she'd moved past began to resurface. "I had an eating disorder in high school that sort of carried over into college, but I had kicked it by graduation. But, when you have an eating disorder, it never really goes away. It's right under the surface, and it's stronger at more stressful times in your life," she explains. "Then, I was

HOW JENNY STAYS POSITIVE UNDER PRESSURE

"When things are really stressful or I'm under a lot of pressure, I like to look back at photos where I know I was at my happiest. It's pretty clear to me which photos show true joy and contentment and which are hiding things under the surface. My smile is the giveaway. I have a smile that's big and full and confident when I'm really, truly happy and content. And then I have a kind of half-smile that's definitely not as full of joy when I'm not. Most of the really happy moments and memories are also some of my least 'perfect' moments. They are spontaneous, and I'm surrounded by other people who give me joy. These photos remind me what really matters . . . loving people through imperfections."

thrown into this incredibly competitive environment where I was working with beautiful women who cared a lot about their appearances. So, I started to care more about my appearance . . . and what I was eating."

Even if you've never struggled with food, at some point, you've probably had a front-row seat to the toxic ways that some women compete with one another—for assignments, attention, men . . . and often, to be thin. It can be hard for even the most confident chicks to opt out of the race to the bottom.

"There was a time when all those girls were juicing, and that was the beginning for me. They were talking about their juices and not eating, and I was sitting next to them thinking, 'Stop talking about this! I don't want to hear about it!' They were all excited to juice and not eat, and eventually, I felt like, oh, I need to do this too," Jenny says. And so she'd skip lunch or not eat dinner. She'd think obsessively about food and binge-watch the Food Network.

"For me, it was about control. Food was the one area of my life where I felt I could have complete control. I didn't have control over my finances. I could barely make rent. I didn't have control over my job. I was working long hours. When you're working for someone else, you don't really have control over your own life."

After a few months, as she learned the ropes, her life came into balance, and Jenny started to feel less frantic. The pace of the job became manageable and the self-destructive impulses started to become background noise. But then, as if she was punishing herself for getting too comfortable, she slipped again into the darkness. "Am I meant to be here? Am I good enough for this job? What makes me, a girl from the Midwest who grew up in the suburbs, good enough?" Jenny says she remembers thinking. "Maybe if I lose weight or look better or become a smaller size, that will make me deserve this more."

Jenny knew she needed help. Therapy was more than she could afford, even with insurance. And so she turned to friends and a trusted religious mentor.

"I had a few girlfriends who supported me, and we talked about finding value outside of work," she says. "I wanted to do a good job because that was important to me, but I had to learn how to find joy and fulfillment outside of work too."

LETTING YOURSELF LOSE ALL CONTROL

Some women are so in control all the time that the only way they can duck from the pressure is to surrender and lose all control. Jade works 80 to 100 hours a week in investment banking—and she loves every hyperintense moment. At 24, she is in the room advising CEOs about multibillion-dollar deals. It's the kind of power that gives her an edge over her high-flying friends at Facebook or Google, who won't be making those kinds of decisions for another 15 to 20 years—and she loves that too. She was a Division 1 lacrosse player, and she thrives on competition.

In her day-to-day job, there's no room to sit back and take a breath, and with that level of intensity, sometimes the idea of letting herself go is kind of appealing. "Your day is so serious and so structured and intense that you just want to fling over to the opposite end of the spectrum," she explains. "The thinking is, I made money; I worked hard. Let's go crazy." The hard-work culture easily transitions to hard partying.

"There's 'let's party and get fucked up,' and then there's the 'I'm here till 3:00 a.m., I need to get my work done, so I'm abusing drugs,'" Jade says, explaining the finance culture she's seen. "It's Adderall—a lot of Adderall. Cocaine and Vyvanse. People talk about it openly. And the cocaine people brag about how much blow they did in a weekend." She admits that she's been one of those people. After a few months on the job, she found herself with a regular after-work cocaine habit. "Sometimes, I wake up and think, 'What are you doing with your life?'" Jade says. "Sometimes, I feel invincible. It's either, *that was fucking awesome* or *I hate myself.*"

During those low moments with no real validation on the job, Jade also found herself chasing hookups that she hoped would make her feel better but only made her feel worse. "You're thinking, 'I don't feel good about myself, so I want someone else to make me feel good.' As soon as that turns into looking for someone to fill an emptiness, that's when it becomes unhealthy. And then the day after, you punish yourself. You think you should be better than that. If you think so highly of yourself, why are you letting yourself be used like that? Maybe you really are worthless."

Jade is still in the work-hard, party-hard culture, but she's learned to find more balance. She's stopped drinking hard liquor, she's taking a dance class (something she used to love), she's making time for dates, and she has a dinner club of women in her industry who understand the intense pressure she's under. But even with all those out-of-control nights and crap mornings, Jade wouldn't dial down this part of her Big Life. "If I went back and told my 21-year-old self, 'This is what it's going to be like—get ready,' it may have been helpful. But I was told how hard the culture was, and I didn't listen. The truth is that until you're in it, you don't know how dark it can get."

> TIPS FROM CHICKS
> AT THE TABLE
> ———
> ## HOW JADE KEEPS DARKNESS AT BAY
>
> "I work 16- to 18-hour days 6 days a week, and I pretty much don't leave my desk except to get lunch or go to the bathroom—sometimes I forget to pee. But every evening, I leave work, go to the gym, lift weights, and listen to the dubstep station on Pandora, and then go back and finish work. That's my release."

WHEN THE PRESSURE LEADS TO SELF-SABOTAGE

Many women around my table have been brave enough to open up about their destructive behaviors. These women tend to talk about their disorders as something separate, as if they're describing a part of themselves that has a mind of its own and yells at them, shouting out the most destructive messages imaginable: *You're a loser. You don't deserve to be* normal. *You don't have what it takes.* The worst part is that if you listen to these messages for long enough, you start to believe they are true.

I've written a lot about the dark side in my career. It's an important conversation to have with teens and young women who get their legs knocked out from beneath them by the first signs of emotional distress or psychological trauma, which they have no skills to cope with. Binge eating, withholding food, forced vomiting, obsessive eating habits, habitual binge drinking, prescription drug abuse, painkiller addiction, cutting—it's a sliding scale from experimentation to self-sabotage to full-blown self-harm. But I've heard again and again from girls and young women that these dangerous behaviors are often a manifestation of a crushing, unrelenting, and unforgiving pressure to be perfect in every way.

When I started working on this book, I didn't expect to find that many of these behaviors trail women into their 20s and 30s. Even behaviors that have been under control for years begin to pop up under pressure. It's a feeling we've all felt to some degree: You need to be the totally confident cool girl who is also superhot. To look fantastic while having a great time *all the time*. To be strong. To be the chick with the great ideas. And the list goes on.

It's worth saying again: It's hard to do big things. Your Big Life matters, and you're emotional about it—of course you are. It's the most important thing. Your frayed nerves and bruised ego probably need more self-care than you have the time to give.

Sometimes, handling it all feels impossible, and there's a voice in your head spewing out the toxic idea that you'll never measure up. Even on good days—when you get a compliment from your boss or take on an exciting new project—you still can't completely escape the feeling that you're not up to standards. Your emotions spin out of control and you feel helpless. Looming deadlines or a simple mistake can eat away at you. You're not sleeping, you're not eating well, and forget about exercise. This anxiety and lack of self-care can land you in a place where seemingly innocent behaviors morph into a dangerous cycle of self-sabotage.

That's the pressure to be perfect.

I'm sure you've had days when you make it into the office just in time. Your hair is brushed and arranged into a twisty knot, the lip gloss you smeared on gives you enough of a glow, and no one would ever guess the cute dress you're wearing was pulled out of the dirty laundry before you ran out of the house. You send a quick text to the friends you were out with until late last night and take a gulp of cold brew, and the real work of your day begins. Countless emails, scheduling, problem solving, last-minute tasks for important meetings or presentations keep you running, and you're hoping you won't screw any of it up. *Again.* Did you remember to reschedule that lunch for your boss? Did you print out the right report? You start second-guessing yourself, and the anxiety starts to creep in. Soon, it's taking up a big space inside you, and you seriously can't understand how you even got this job, or how you haven't been fired yet.

Maybe you look around and see the other chicks in the office. They chat casually and share laughs over their superhealthy salads while you remember that the low-fat yogurt you brought for lunch is still sitting in your purse. It's already 3:00 p.m., so you might as well save all those calories. You'll eat it later—maybe.

Or, maybe the day keeps getting busier and tasks needed to be completed 5 minutes ago. The pressure and anxiety you feel are overwhelming. You text your friends that you definitely want to meet up for drinks tonight. The drinking and partying feels like fun—a great stress-reliever—but then it turns into something else. Maybe you're staying out too late and drinking too much—ensuring you feel like crap the next day and putting you right back in that vulnerable space that made going out again seem like a good idea in the first place.

Maybe you're getting black-out drunk, or having hookups that feel like a welcome distraction but leave you sad about the lack of real connection. Cocktails with girlfriends and easy hookups are one thing. It's another thing entirely when this becomes a cycle of self-punishment, as if you need a reason to listen to that voice in your head—the one that would like you to think you're a loser who doesn't deserve success or love.

> **"When you're feeling pressured about not being perfect at work, then you start trying to be perfect in the other parts of your life."**

It should go without saying that professional help is important when it comes to self-harming behaviors. That being said, it's also my mission to help you see yourself as part of a sisterhood of women who are going through this together. I'm not only talking about the highs—the successes and big achievements—but the lows too. The women who've spoken candidly to me about the pressure to be perfect wanted to do so because they didn't want to hide their experiences. They didn't want to feel alone in their struggles, and

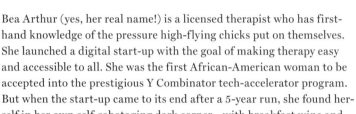

WHEN DO YOU KNOW YOU NEED
PROFESSIONAL HELP?

Bea Arthur (yes, her real name!) is a licensed therapist who has first-hand knowledge of the pressure high-flying chicks put on themselves. She launched a digital start-up with the goal of making therapy easy and accessible to all. She was the first African-American woman to be accepted into the prestigious Y Combinator tech-accelerator program. But when the start-up came to its end after a 5-year run, she found herself in her own self-sabotaging dark corner—with breakfast wine and McDonald's burgers—that she had to climb out of. It's not easy to be honest about the things that feel like personal failures, but Bea says that just talking about the pressures diffuses them and keeps them from building.

"Drinking, sex, drugs, eating, or not eating—all those are distracting behaviors. They might feel good at first, but the sooner you can face the thing that's actually making you feel bad, the sooner you can let go of the things that are only temporarily making you feel better, and are actually making you worse. Look for your triggers: What puts you in that dark and vulnerable place? It usually starts slow. You have a few too many glasses of wine and shortly find that you've been drunk multiple days in a row, or you start a Paleo diet and find that you're now eating just six almonds a day. When you know the cause, you can work to avoid the situations that make you feel worthless. The more you can align yourself with the things that make you feel strong, the things you're good at, the more in control you'll feel. It's all easier said than done, and sometimes you need a therapist to help you get there. The bottom line is that you need professional help when the behaviors start to interfere with your life, such as when you're missing events or avoiding things you used to enjoy and isolating yourself."

they don't want you to feel alone either. While I can't solve these problems for you, it's my hope that this conversation will light the way for other young women who aren't as aware of how their anxieties and ambitions are tangled.

TOXIC BOSSES AND EMOTIONAL VAMPIRES

Sometimes, you don't have to look too deeply to find your triggers—they're in the office next to yours.

Tiffani had wanted to live in Los Angeles ever since she was a little girl. She was proud when she managed to get there from her quiet coastal town, but her work environment wasn't what she expected at all. "I found a horrible job in finance as this guy's assistant. I was dealing with his mistresses and buying them gifts. He would come into the office and scream at me like I was an idiot—because his car wasn't ready or something. Then, the next day, he'd come in with a gift for me from Hermès," she explains. "I cried every day." Tiffani left this job and the tears behind, but she reflects that it seems like her boss was trying to make her feel small. "I think toxic bosses make people cry to feel more empowered themselves. I think they scream because it's intimidating and scary."

Vanessa, who knows she can make a huge impact in the beauty industry, spent years trying to work her way past small-time indie brands and low-level jobs only to land a spot at a huge prestigious firm where her bosses made her feel worthless. "I've cried a lot. It feels like you're in high school again, being talked down to or manipulated," she says. Crying in the bathroom was a sign that she was unraveling. "I think there's a lot of pressure that you're putting on yourself to be successful that's not always just career. Body image and eating disorders are huge. And when work gets tough and you got 3 hours of sleep, it's the first thing your mind goes to as a coping mechanism," she explains. "When you're feeling pressured about not being perfect at work, then you start trying to be perfect in the other parts of your life."

So, how do you keep the pressure to be perfect on the job from infecting your whole life? After all, you can't always quit your job. So how do you keep those dark impulses from taking over?

IF YOU CAN'T QUIT, LEARN TO CARE LESS

You always strive to do your best, but there are times when it feels like no matter what you do, it's not enough. Your boss is bananas, or the company is poorly run; there are instances when you can't combat the dysfunction with trying harder and doing good work. In these situations, sometimes the right approach is to learn how to care less. You can't always quit your job, but you can try to separate all your emotion from it.

Tiffani moved on from her toxic boss as fast as she could. She knew that there was something more she needed to do and someplace safer where she could do it. She could learn the basics of her business anywhere—and so she did. She landed a new job, where critiques of her work didn't feel like personal attacks.

Vanessa couldn't leave her job yet. She needed to have the prestigious company on her résumé for a year or two to help her move to the next level in her career. And so she had to separate herself from what she described as the "emotional vampires." She wrote a memo making a strong business—not personal—case for why she needed to be placed in another department in the company. She couldn't always detach her emotions from the work, but making a plan to take control of the situation helped her maintain equilibrium. And her professional, unemotional approach with her bosses paid off with a customized job in a different department.

It's a sucky feeling when you set standards for yourself and you feel that no matter how high you jump, you don't get close to reaching them. Something is always in your way. But, if you're holding back tears at your desk and constantly walking on eggshells, it might be time to detach from the drama and chaos. Your boss screams at you that you lost the company an account because there was a minor typo on page 63 of a report, what's wrong with you, and what were you thinking? Okay, you'll be more careful next time. But just because he can't keep things in perspective doesn't mean you can't.

A mistake is a mistake. It's not a reflection of your competence, character, or worth as a human being. You definitely can't do a good job at work if you can't take care of yourself, and it's hard to take care of yourself when you're bombarded by messages in the office that you're not good enough. Those moments are hard, but this isn't the right job for you. Your Big Career is still ahead—so for now, remember that this job isn't your whole life! Focus on the thought that there's something much bigger that you were meant to do—and until that job manifests, care less.

THE DOUBLE LIFE

We're living in an age of total transparency, and while some Badass Babes wouldn't think twice about telling their bosses that they're working from home because they have terrible period cramps, there's still a lot of secrecy around struggle. Sure, you talk about your therapist—everyone seems to have one, and it's a bit of a badass badge of honor to say you're working so hard that you need that hour to focus on yourself. But you don't mention the hard work you have to do every day to stay strong. You want everyone to think that your life is as lovely as the pretty one you display to the world on Instagram.

Jasmine has put up that kind of pretty front for *years*. "I had my first panic attack onstage at my saxophone concert when I was 10," she says. "In 10th grade, I became restrictive bulimic—we'd just moved towns, I started a new school, and I was a year behind in math. I'd always been at the top of my class before that."

Jasmine started therapy in high school, and while it helped her handle the anxiety, it was still there, forcing her to push harder and harder.

"I was so type A. In high school, I took every Advanced Placement class you could take. I was top of my class, obsessed with college," she says. "I was always terrified of not doing the best I could to get to whatever the next step was. I was so blinded by how anxious I was that it took me a long time to notice the actual ambition. I never had a moment to stop and think, 'What do I want? What is the end game?'"

Jasmine plowed past those questions and pushed herself into a rigorous college course load with one goal: achieve.

But during junior year, when her boyfriend found her uncon-scious after she chased her antidepressant meds with a bot-tle of tequila, she was finally forced to face that she needed in-patient treatment.

Now 24, Jasmine is proud to be working at her first full-time job at a research firm. But she refuses to hide her past.

The secrecy can do even more damage, she says. "I think a lot of people are surprised when I'm open about this stuff, and that bothers me. I've come to realize that more people struggle with anxiety in some form than you would ever think. I wish people were more open about it. Anxiety shouldn't have to be hidden. It can really help to know that you're able to tell your story. And when you do, you're bringing other people along for the ride. It always helps to know you're not alone."

PERFECTION IS THE ENEMY OF AMBITION

It's not your ambition that's leading to self-doubt and self-sabotaging behavior. But it's hard to deny that, for many chicks, ambition and anxiety go hand and hand. When Jas-mine's anxiety was taking over, she took some time off, sought treatment, and learned about what she needs to do to stay healthy. "I learned to hate the word *perfect*. Nothing is per-fect. No one is perfect," she says.

The pressure to be perfect is immense—and Jasmine wisely recognizes that the thinking will always be there. "The disordered thinking is what doesn't go away. It's probably always going to be with me in some shape or form," she admits. "The important thing is that you tell your story. You don't have to come all the way through it. I'm still going through it, but now I know there are other people along for the ride. You don't have to come through it with a big bang. It's a gradual process, and you just have to keep going."

It's a powerful message: You just have to keep going. Nothing is perfect. No one is perfect. And this process of building a Big Life is messy and hard, but amazingly rewarding. It doesn't matter whether or not you come out on top—you simply have to keep moving. Every day, put one foot in front of the other. It might not be perfect, but it's good enough.

10

THE

BIG LIFE

FOR ALL

WHAT I'VE LEARNED
FROM YOU

Not long ago, I gave a talk to a women's group in Providence, Rhode Island. Before I went on, the volunteer who brought me bagels and kept me company backstage told me a bit about her journey. She graduated from college with a degree in international business and had scored a coveted internship with Disney. Her dad had connections at a company based in Berlin, and she knew a job there would mean a killer starting salary. It was exciting to be at the beginning of her Big Life, but she was starting to have a different vision for herself. A year of travel, she thought, would give her a broader perspective on the world. When she returned, she planned to launch a nonprofit that tapped into her passion, while she cooked up an even bigger international corporate job on the side. She was such an amazing example of the changing way young women see the possibilities for themselves in the world that I mentioned her in my speech that day.

Then, during the Q&A session, a woman stood up in the back of the room. She was probably in her mid-40s, and neatly dressed for a Saturday. She wasn't there as someone's mom or as a mentor; she was there for information, just like all the other young women in the room.

"It seems like millennials are all anyone can talk about," she said. "How can someone like me, who is not at the beginning of her career, not get lost in the conversation?"

She cut right to the emotional core. I've heard this feeling of anxiety come out in different ways: Senior execs who roll their eyes and complain that their millennial employees are lazy, distracted, and disloyal. Well-meaning advisors who want me to teach you how to fall in line with the old-school hierarchy they built rather than disrupt it. Business leaders who adopt a jargony way of speaking to connect with their younger employees. This is all about fear of being edged out of a massive national conversation about the way work is changing and how you're changing it.

And it's not a totally irrational fear. Change is hard—for everyone. You're finding yourself butting up against old ways of doing things and senior execs with a traditional POV who don't respect your fresh approach. They're frustrated that the foundation they built their careers on is moving under their feet and that their years of experience and hard-won expertise isn't always valued.

On that morning in Rhode Island, in that moment, both sides were united with a common goal: to make their mark on the world and to build their own Big Life.

"You have a choice," I said, addressing the whole audience, at any age, "to feel diminished or to be inspired. I choose inspired."

There's a realization across the board that the idea of work and ambition is changing—particularly for women. That a job doesn't have to mean working at an office. That being candid with your colleagues and coworkers about what you're getting paid can help everyone negotiate more strongly. That the word *ambition* is something we should *own* and normalize, rather than debate whether or not it has negative connotations. That a side hustle can be as meaningful in moving your career along or giving you deeper meaning when you're 45 as it can when you're 25.

My best friend is president of the PTA at her daughter's school and controls a $500,000 budget. She runs it like a small business, and it's giving her skills that she doesn't get much opportunity to flex in her job as a corporate attorney. It's a huge bonus that she's making her daughter's school better too.

To help in her salary negotiations, a colleague who was up

for a Big Job reached out to ask me to ballpark what I had been paid. We had worked together years earlier, and back then—when it probably would have helped us both add more money to our small bank accounts—she would never have thought to ask. But the kind of transparency that's second nature to you isn't TMI; it's smart business for everyone.

Every day that I've sat in my coworking space writing this book, I've watched a woman I know greet her young team before breezing into a conference room. She had a bigwig corporate job, but she wanted to see if she could make it on her own. As she was building her business, she was also building her family—she has an adorable baby who often comes into work with her. She's working like a maniac, but she's creating something of her own. And even if she's working at 11:00 p.m. or 7:30 a.m. to please a client, she has the flexibility to see her son during the day or take long weekends with her husband. That's enviable at any age.

The advice I gave that 40-something woman that morning in Providence is the same advice I give you. This moment of change in the world is your opportunity to make your life bigger instead of letting the force of change make you feel small and overwhelmed. You have the choice to be the architect of change or to let change happen to you. Take the reins.

THE BIG LIFE:
WHAT WE CAN ALL LEARN

I am honored to have had a front-row seat for the revolution: during my 15 years in teen and young women's media, as a reporter who had the honor of interviewing some of the most powerful women and the smartest thought leaders, and most recently, in personal conversations around my dining room table. It's all been a drumroll leading up to this moment in history when women have never had a bigger opportunity to craft the lives they want. *On their own terms.* And while it might seem that it's every generation's duty to rewrite the rules to work for them, it hasn't always been that way. When Gen Xers like me were faced with a recession and a disastrous job market, instead of carving a new path or creating new businesses out of college, we followed the trend toward "McJobs"—low-paying gigs at McDonald's or coffee shops that were meant to hold us over until the economy right-sided. We celebrated slacker culture. (Have you Netflixed *Reality Bites*? Winona Ryder, Gen X icon, chooses goateed Ethan Hawke over buttoned-up Ben Stiller. That's how my generation reacted to their opportunity to take control.) And the generation that came of age while the economy was booming in the early 2000s—think Kim Kardashian—used their moment to celebrate affluence rather than the meaning you're demanding in everything you do.

This moment is not just yours; it's everyone's chance to rewrite the rules.

You might be fresh out of college and about to take that exciting first step, or maybe you've landed a big promotion. Perhaps you have loads of experience and much to offer the world, like the woman who came to see me in Rhode Island. Wherever you are, this conversation is for you, and here are a few things we can all take away from it.

RELATIONSHIPS ARE EVERYTHING

Working so hard to make your mark on the world can be isolating, don't you think? You're trying to carve out a place for yourself, trying to learn the rules at work, and also trying to make up a few of your own so the job works on your terms too. You can't always lean on your coworkers—you still need to be professional with them. Your parents probably don't get all the subtle nuances of your business that are so important to you, and when you're with your friends, you just want to drink wine and gossip about *The Bachelor*.

The dinners around my table have been important because they've allowed Badass Babes in different jobs, different industries, and different stages of their lives to connect around the shared threads of ambition.

The importance of connection became crystal clear to me during one dinner in particular. Two of the women had dated briefly, but after they broke up, one of them met the love of her life—and she was there too. They invited a work friend to dinner that night, but you'd never know that she hadn't been part of their squad from the beginning—that's how close they seemed. It was clear these chicks were devoted to one another. They clinked glasses in celebration. They held one another's hands during complicated confessions. They play-punched one another's arms during some silly ribbing. They jumped in to share memories and viewpoints for one another during tricky questions. These women had a shared vision for how they wanted the world to work for them. This was not a manufactured network. This was *sisterhood*. And they were invested not only in each other's work but also in each other's lives.

Without these kinds of close bonds, dreams feel empty, and ambition feels cold and calculating. You want to know that someone you care about, and who cares about you in return, is witnessing your transformation from a girl with a dream to a woman with her own power to flex in the world. If there's no one to share it with, it's like it doesn't really happen, right?

I was deeply moved by the connection between Chelsea and her husband, Trevor. They'd met at a Halloween party in college when she was dressed as a Spice Girl and he was a pirate. They'd crafted a life together—taking turns doing whatever was necessary to support each other's dreams. She got a boring but lucrative corporate job while he was in law school. He supported her when she took a huge risk on a start-up. They moved cities three times for their jobs or families: LA to DC to San Francisco to New York. They'd literally grown up together, but they'd allowed each other to grow in his or her own direction as well. She looks at him intently as he speaks, and he is equally rapt when she voices an opinion. It's not just #RelationshipGoals, but an actual relationship—give and take.

When I met my husband at 35 years old, I had a career I'd built from scratch and a job I loved. I was confident in my ability to live a life of fun and adventure on my own. But together, we made plans and built a family, and our vision for our potential in the world got so much bigger. The more we share our hopes and dreams with the people around us, the deeper and more meaningful those connections become. And the more we're there to celebrate or commiserate with family and friends who become like family, the more powerful our power becomes.

You might think that the relationships you're forming now are transitory—everyone is hustling and moving in different directions all at once. And yes, some friendships will fade away. But there is still value in learning from people who aren't destined to be lifelong connections. I call it the New Best Friend—someone you instantly fall in line with. Everything she says is hilarious, amazing, and insightful. You're totally aligned in this one moment—until you're not. The harder you fall for the New Best Friend, the faster the friendship usually flames out. But you always come away a little smarter, a little more fun, with your life enriched in ways big and small.

Many of the connections you're making now will be long-lasting. It's hard to know when you're first starting out that the people you're coming up with in the world now are the people you're going to continue to encounter throughout your career, and throughout your life. Even if you didn't have Facebook to remind you that it's the birthday of the girl who sat next to you during your internship, she's likely to be at the same industry events, work for the same clients, know friends of a friend, and be a connection. When you realize that life and business are long, you'll feel like the work you're putting in now is worth it and not just for the moment.

BE PURPOSEFUL IN BUILDING YOUR LIFE

I'm at a fairly senior level in my career, but I'm relatively new to being a mom. At my house, we're still working through sleepless nights and coordinating school drop-offs and playdates. So I loved the Badass Babes dinner that gave me a chance to bond with other new moms who also had demanding jobs to navigate. I was struck by how these women had purposefully crafted their Big Lives with partners and kids, while keeping their dreams for themselves front and center.

Victoria, 34, is a high-powered VP at a start-up that was acquired for major money. She has an adorable toddler daughter and admits that she's already working on baby number two; ideally, she'd like to have three or four. She also has her sights set on being CEO someday. Maybe she'll start something new, maybe she'll helm an existing company, but she knows she wants to put herself in a position to run a significant business. For now, as a young mother with a booming career, she knows exactly what she needs to make this happen: She wants to figure out how to work at a higher level, taking on more responsibility while working fewer hours. She's going to level up and work smarter rather than harder, and she's determined to find a way to do it on her own terms.

Kelly, 33, put the pieces of her life into place one by one. Right as she and her husband were about to buy a pricey house in LA, they realized the big mortgage, and the work pressure that came with it, weren't how they wanted to start their lives together. They had a vision for how they wanted to raise a family. So they moved to Hawaii, where she got a job based in New York that allowed her to work remotely, and they had a son. It's a complicated formula, but it was put together carefully. Kelly wasn't simply going with the flow and seeing what happened; she and her husband came up with these goals together.

These women have an eye on what's coming next and an idea about how to get there. They aren't taking a random walk through life; they're walking with purpose. And if that purpose changes from time to time? That's fine. They still have an idea about what they're ultimately after, and they know they can get it.

While I've always dreamed big, I've never had an endgame—I've always kept my eyes open for new opportunities. I've always looked around to see what could be next. You can't always see three steps ahead, but you should think about how the role or the relationship you're in now can help lead to something else, and how that fits into your big vision for yourself.

THE LITTLE SECRETS CAN MATTER THE MOST

It's funny, the things that stick in your brain. Elizabeth, who hustled her way to New York from New Mexico, confesses that the cute Milly frock she's wearing to meet up with me is part of her Rent the Runway unlimited plan. For $139 a month, she has a new outfit customized for every occasion: meetings, dates, dinners. She doesn't have to think about what she's going to wear. Or wonder if it's clean of if she's worn it to the same event before. New outfits arrive at her front door three times a week, so she can just show up looking great.

Grace always has a clean dress hanging in her office closet and a pair of heels under her desk. Not that you'd ever catch her looking anything but put-together. But it's a trick she learned on her first day at her corporate job, when she showed up in some cool-girl jogging pants and then unexpectedly had to join the CEO for a fancy dinner. She had to run out to Banana Republic and drop $150 she didn't have on a new dress—after that, she vowed to be prepared for anything.

I've always said that casual Friday is a scam. Inevitably, you're going to get called to a client meeting, have to represent your research, or run into your boss's boss in the elevator.

No matter how cute your jeans, that level of casualness will undermine your authority.

Don't be fooled. These are not fashion and beauty secrets; they are *success secrets*. No one can feel like the true badass she really is when she's walking into a room tugging on her shirt because she's worried her outfit is all wrong, or she keeps glancing at herself in the mirror because she thinks her hair is too frizzy. It's all too easy to obsess over minor details like chipped nails when you're stressed about the major ones . . . like giving a killer presentation or asking for a new assignment. Make taking care of the basics like planning your outfits or making a regular mani appointment part of your routine, and you can turn your focus to the big picture.

LEARN FROM THE WRONG TURNS

You have to celebrate your wins, but remember that you can learn just as much from wrong turns and bad decisions. There's no shame in screwing up. The path you're forging is a tricky one. Everyone's perspective can get wacky on occasion. Learn, move on, and remind yourself that every bad situation is an opportunity to reward yourself with grit and resilience.

- One ambitious babe was so competitive with the other women in her office that every success they achieved felt like something was taken away from her. You have to keep your eyes on your own paper.
- One ballsy woman saw dates as a running tally of how much she'd spent on bikini waxes and blow-

drys versus how much he was spending on drinks and dinner. You can't make a meaningful connection if you're counting the dollars.

- One hard-charging attorney was incredibly proud of her accomplishments—her Big Job and big salary meant her husband could go back to school to get his MBA. However, she repeatedly said that she wished he would give up his plan to "find himself" and just get a job. The rules of relationships have changed, and I have cheered the women who actively aim to be the breadwinners in their families. But it will never work if you feel resentful of the new dynamic.

- One chick was so excited about the buzzy start-up where she'd landed a year out of school. But her enthusiasm clouded her judgment when the company lost its office lease and had to move all the office equipment into her tiny apartment while it hunted for a new space. No one wants to see the copy machine first thing in the morning. Even worse, the boss had no boundaries and made a pass at her after one happy hour. When she rejected him, he sidelined her to being a personal assistant. I'm all for start-ups, but don't throw your judgment out the window because you're forging new territory. And beware the company with no human resources department!

All these women recovered from their missteps, learned a little something, and had a good story to tell over cocktails. And the truth is that those mistakes helped them take their next steps with more self-awareness and confidence.

YOUR VISION GROWS WITH YOU

When I first met Olivia, she was dating indie rockers who either worshipped her or broke her heart. She was out partying five nights a week and giving her best friend a hard time if she wanted to turn in early to rest up for a meeting or deadline. Olivia had a vision for herself, but in that moment, she was prioritizing fun. Fast-forward a year and she came for dinner again. She had a new job with increasing responsibility. She felt important and included, and it showed—not only in the cute Chanel flats she could afford to rock but also in the way she carried herself. And this time, she had traded the rock guys for dudes in medical school—not that they were necessarily better boyfriends, but they had life plans beyond their next gig, and they were less likely to text her to come out for a drink at 1:00 a.m. As her vision for herself started to change at work, her vision for herself changed in her personal life too. As one part of your life evolves, so do other parts, and the pieces start to better fit together.

Sometimes, the evolution isn't slow and steady. A dramatic move can shake up your world and nothing is ever the same. When her father had a life-threatening illness, Melissa knew she needed to learn how to be self-sufficient and prepare for the day he wouldn't be there for her. She bought a one-way ticket to Argentina, daring herself to make it on her own. There, she taught English to schoolkids, and that experience convinced her to come back to the U.S. and become a teacher. She'd found her purpose and her self-reliance in one swoop.

And sometimes, you force a change in your life to propel yourself further, faster. I recently got an email from a young woman asking for advice about moving cross-country. Her company was embroiled in a huge public scandal, and she felt tainted by the rift in her corporate culture. She was single and financially strapped by school loans, and worried about New York City's high rent. She wanted a clean start. She was asking me for job-search advice. But, what she really wanted was validation that her struggle would be worth it. She wanted to know how to overcome the friction of her current situation and start living the bigger vision she had for herself. Even if her Dream Job wasn't on the other side of that cross-country move, seeing the world from a different city changes your perspective so that you can make new plans for yourself.

I used to get letters from girls who said that *Seventeen* had changed and they were disappointed in us. It's true, the magazine was always evolving, but it hadn't changed in the way they thought; *they'd* changed. They'd moved on, grown up, and outgrown the mag. They couldn't see it because *Seventeen* had been so important in their lives, but I could. They'd conquered the acne, period problems, and guy drama that loomed so large in their early teen years, and they'd moved on. You have the same kind of conquering on your horizon too. When you honor the hard work you've done to get to this new level in your life—at any age—and let go of old ideas of who you were or who you think you should be, you get a clearer vision of who you *want* to be.

IT'S YOUR STORY, SO MAKE IT AMAZING

In the end, here's what I've learned from writing this book, from talking to so many women, and from my years of growing up and growing together with you: The stories we tell—to other women and to ourselves—matter. That story that started with random thoughts and ideas is blossoming into a full-blown adventure, and you will always control the narrative. You have a choice to see the twists and turns of your path as an exciting expedition or a disaster waiting to happen. The challenges ahead could be a reason to celebrate or a cause for concern. You decide if you're going to tell stories about chasing the newness or how you found solace on well-worn paths.

Ultimately, you are the hero of your story. And it is an essential part of becoming who you were meant to be. The best part: You never stop becoming. With every story, your life is becoming better, happier, smarter, more interesting, and *bigger* than anything you could have ever imagined.

#TheBigLife

ACKNOWLEDGMENTS

This book would still be an idea hastily scribbled on a Post-It stashed in the back of my desk drawer without the candor and openness of the women who gathered around my dinner table and huddled with me over mid-afternoon coffees. And so first and foremost, I send my love and admiration to all the Badass Babes who have shared their hopes and dreams and fears with me. I am in awe of your power and forever grateful for your sisterhood. The world is yours for the taking.

I owe a special thanks to Michelle Phan, who was so deeply connected to the mission of this book that she secretly made me cry over the phone when we talked about the possibilities for it to make a change in the world. I am honored to have your support.

Jennifer Hyman, Alexa von Tobel, Alicia Menendez, Tammy Tibbetts, and Gabi Gregg are the ultimate squad. You are each crafting your Big Life in superlative style, and I have learned so much from your example.

When you have a tricky question, ask a Badass Babe. And

no one is more badass than Carmen Lilly, Alexandra Dickinson, and Bea Arthur—you are truth-tellers.

Meaghan O'Connor and Hannah Orenstein did phenomenal research. Thank you for returning all my early-morning and late night emails with even the most random and weirdly specific questions.

I am lucky to have a bench of amazing authors who shared their tips, tricks, and insider secrets, so thank you to Tiffany Dufu, Jessica Bennett, Kate White, Aliza Licht, Paula Rizzo, and Farnoosh Torabi.

I could not ask for a more generous publishing and editing team than at Rodale. I love that you have such a positive and optimistic outlook on making women's lives more meaningful. I am lucky to have worked with Jennifer Levesque, Isabelle Hughes, Angie Giammarino, Yelena Nesbit, Aly Mostel, Emily Weber Eagan, Jeffrey Batzli, and Amy King.

I owe a very special shout-out to my editor, Marisa Vigilante, whose steady hand, clear vision, and vast reserves of patience helped make *The Big Life* even bigger.

I am deeply indebted to my agent, Brandi Bowles at Foundry Literary + Media, who believed in this book, pushed me to go even deeper, and then expertly shepherded the project into the right hands. And also to agent Richie Kern, who instantly saw untapped possibilities for *The Big Life*.

Paula Balzer was the most talented and devoted writing partner, who deeply believes in the power of young women and wants everyone to live their Big Life on their own terms. Thank you for always adding extra sugar.

Publicity powerhouse Dee Dee DeBartlo brought boundless energy and big, booming ideas.

I need one more moment to thank my mom and dad,

Roslyn and Daniel Shoket, who saw me looking out my teen-age bedroom window and helped me imagine a life that was bigger than anything I could see around me.

Sometimes, the people to whom you owe the greatest thanks are the ones who are hardest to honor. I would never have been able to make this book a reality without the love and endless support of my husband, Richard Goozée, who was 100 percent behind this project, even when it was just a hastily written idea on a Post-It note in the back of my drawer. And although they are not old enough to read this acknowl-edgment, my heart belongs to my kids, Leonardo and Isabel, who jumped on the couch to entertain at my dinners, were (happily) kept up past their bedtime when the conversations stretched into the late hours, and are the sweetest reminders of what matters most in *my* Big Life.

ABOUT THE AUTHOR

© ANNE MENKE

ANN SHOKET has been a key architect in shaping the national conversation about and for millennial women. Her mission is to help young women feel so confident that they can walk into any room and own it. As the editor-in-chief of *Seventeen* from 2007 to 2014, Shoket repositioned the iconic fashion and beauty brand to dominate as the most relevant voice for its 13 million readers and drove it to become number one on every platform. *Forbes* named her one of the "Most Powerful Fashion Magazine Editors" in the country. Shoket has appeared regularly on *Good Morning America*, *Today*, *The Oprah Winfrey Show*, *The View*, CNN, *Access Hollywood*, and *E! News*, and she was a guest judge for four seasons on *America's Next Top Model*.